Schoolhouse Planning

Co-Editors

Karl V. Hertz, Ed.D.
Superintendent
Mequon-Thiensville School District
Mequon, Wisconsin

C. William Day, Partner
Educational Planning Associates
Bloomington, Indiana

Association of School Business Officials International

1987 BOARD OF DIRECTORS
EXECUTIVE COMMITTEE

President
Dr. Jack D. Oatley, RSBA
Assoc. Supt. for Admin. Services
Kent Intermediate School Dist.
2650 E. Beltline SE
Grand Rapids, MI 49506
616/949-7270

President-Elect
S. Fred Hawkins, RSBA
Asst. Supt. of Finance & Operations
Kirkwood R-7 Schools
11289 Manchester Road
Kirkwood, MO 63122
314/965-9510

Past President
H. Ronald Smith, RSBA
Business Administrator
Essex County Vocational Schools
68 South Harrison Street
East Orange, NJ 07018
201/676-0955

Vice President
Donna R. Gloshen, RSBA
Business Manager
Educational Serv. Unit 3
4224 South 133rd Street
Omaha, NE 68137
402/330-2770

Executive Director
Ronald A. Allen, CAE
ASBO Headquarters
1760 Reston Avenue/Suite 411
Reston, VA 22090
703/478-0405

DIRECTORS

1985-87

Gerald B. Brashears, RSBA
Asst. Supt./Business Services
Abilene Independent Sch. Dist.
842 North Mockingbird/Box 981
Abilene, TX 79604
915/677-1444

Donald C. Mercure, RSBO
Business Manager
South Windsor Public Schools
1737 Main Street
South Windsor, CT 06074
203/528-9711

1986-88

Dr. E. Rabon Rodgers, RSBA
Assoc. Supt. for Finance
Richland County Sch. Dist. #2
6831 Brookfield Road
Columbia, SC 29206
803/787-1910

Paul F. Swinford, RSBA
Treasurer
Valley View Schools 365/U
755 Luther Drive
Romeoville, IL 60441
815/886-2707, Ext. 104

1987-89

John (Jack) H. Morris, CA, RSBA
Supt. of Bus. & Treas.
London Board of Education
P.O. Box 5888 1250 Dundas Street
London ON Canada N6A 5L1
519/452-2023

William H. Sullivan, RSBA
Asst. Supt. for Business
N. Rockland Central Schl. Dist.
117 Main Street
Stony Point, NY 10980
914/942-2700

1986-88 Chairman, ASBO Exhibitors' Advisory Committee
Kenneth W. Dahlager, V.P. Sales
Smith System Manufacturing Co.
P.O. Box 64515
St. Paul, MN 55164
612/636-3560

Schoolhouse Planning
Copyright © 1987 by the Association of School
Business Officials International

Printed in the United States of America (002872M)

For more information or to purchase additional copies contact:

ASBO INTERNATIONAL
1760 Reston Avenue, Suite 411
Reston, Virginia 22090
703-478-0405

ISBN No. 0-910170-50-9

Contents

Introduction / 5

Chapter One / 7
Conducting a Feasibility Study
G. Lawson Drinkard, III

Chapter Two / 15
Developing the Master Plan
Gaylaird Christopher

Chapter Three / 21
Writing Educational Specifications
John H. Fredrickson

Chapter Four / 27
Selection of an Architect
Wallace Underwood

Chapter Five / 31
School Site Selection
Ken Falkinham

Chapter Six / 37
Spaces for Learning
Timothy Brown

Chapter Seven / 43
Building Interiors
Dawn R. Day

Chapter Eight / 51
Visual Environment
Kenneth K. Kaestner

Chapter Nine / 57
Fiscal Planning for Building Projects
Lloyd E. Frohreich

Chapter Ten / 65
Construction Management Services
C. E. Haltenhoff

Chapter Eleven / 73
   Construction Observation
   Douglas L. Johnson

Chapter Twelve / 77
   Construction Administration
   Stephen Friedlaender

Chapter Thirteen / 85
   Building Remodeling
   Ronald E. Barnes and Richard Diaz

Chapter Fourteen / 89
   Relocatable Classrooms: A New Approach
   Robert E. Cascaddan, Thomas E. Ewart, and James L. Schott

Introduction

Schoolhouse Planning highlights the pertinent topics related to the planning and construction of educational facilities. It is intended as a relatively modest but straightforward look at the key features of planning educational facilities. The editors have attempted to draw upon the specific areas of expertise of the authors of each chapter. This planning tool is to be used as a guideline in the planning, design, remodeling and construction of educational facilities. The organization of the subject matter presented in this guide is intended to focus on practice rather than theory.

The book starts by dealing with the feasibility study and developing the master plan in the first two chapters. In chapter three the author details the important topic of writing the educational specifications before turning to the selection of the architect in chapter four. Site selection is the order of business for chapter five. The next three chapters deal with spaces for learning, interiors, and the visual environment.

The next four chapters deal with the very important issues of financing, construction management and construction observation and administration. In the next two chapters the authors focus attention upon two rather unique topics which are remodeling and the challenges of building schools in a rapidly growing population.

What have we attempted to achieve in this guide? Hopefully, the sincere efforts of our authors will open new avenues of inquiry to practitioners and to scholars as they deal with the topic of schoolhouse planning. We hope to have provided better cognitive maps from which strategies for management can be developed. We will be pleased if school administrators find that the following pages provide them with a handbook and guidelines to successfully make their way through the potentially thorny experience of planning educational facilities.

Karl V. Hertz, Ed.D., Superintendent
Mequon-Thienville School District
Meguon, Wisconsin

Chapter 1.
Conducting a Feasibility Study

G. Lawson Drinkard, III, AIA*

There are two essential components which must be included in any feasibility study of educational buildings. The first component is the educational program, which describes current and future educational goals and objectives. The second is the architectural feasibility study, which outlines building and renovation possibilities so that the educational goals can be met.

Educational Program

Although the development of educational programs and specifications will be explained in a later chapter, one cannot begin an explanation of how to conduct a school feasibility study without stressing how important this first component is in the planning process. A commitment to educational goals is measurable by the resources—time, staff, money, and space—allocated to achieving these goals. Any school buildings, groups of buildings, or a campus which is well designed must address those program needs which must be satisfied for the educational goals to be met. A well-conceived educational program provides a standard against which existing facilities can be measured. Thus the school space planning consultant should begin his or her work with a well-stated educational program. This educational program should start with a statement of educational philosophy. Some questions which should be asked and then addressed in the development of an educational program include:
 1. What is the primary purpose of this school? What is its educational mission?
 2. To what is the school system committed? Is this commitment correct for the educational mission?

---

*G. Lawson Drinkard, III is a principal in the firm of VMDO Architects, Charlottesville, Virginia.

3. How should learning occur in the school? What kind of teaching methods will help this learning occur?
4. What are the proper roles of students, teachers, administrators, and parents?
5. What kind of spaces are needed for the educational mission to be successful? Are there optional solutions? How many students will/ should be accommodated?

This statement of philosophy will lead to an outline of goals—an "academic blueprint"—which will provide the planner with the facts and figures required to address current and future spatial needs. The success of all future physical planning is dependent upon the care executed in articulating the educational philosophy of the school system and upon the recommended ways the school staff intend to accomplish the goals.

Architectural Feasibility

Architectural feasibility deals with physical space and is usually performed in conjunction with or after an educational assessment is done and an educational program is in place. The architectural feasibility study takes the desired program and studies its physical (building and space) implications.

Issues to be studied vary depending on specific situations; however, the typical architectural feasibility study of an existing educational building (or group of buildings) includes the following:

1. *Statement of Desired Physical Planning Goals*

    This important first step too often is not done. It is important to agree on, and for your consultant to understand, the goals—political, economic, educational, spiritual, physical, etc.

    The goals may be the result of complex educational or political issues, or they may be fairly simple spatial ones such as "we want this open classroom school to be re-planned to accommodate more traditional individual classrooms." Whatever the goals of the study are, they must be stated and written down so that the plan (and the planner) can be evaluated at the end of the study. For instance, were the goals of the study accomplished?

2. *Assessment of Existing Buildings and Spaces*

    An inventory of existing buildings always reveals interesting and often unknown aspects of campus space. If nothing else, an inventory tells a planner what is available and what is not—data which may not have been known or documented.

Depending on the scope of the study, some or all of the following aspects of the existing building(s) should be studied:

a) Structural Condition

Is the building structurally sound and safe? Will it accept additions or alterations? What is its expected "life-span"?

Depending on the age and condition of the building, this may be a simple visual examination or may require more in-depth examination and exploration; ergo, concrete core samples may have to be taken or floor material may have to be removed to investigate structural systems. These factors will, of course, affect both the time required to perform the study and its cost.

b) Mechanical and Electrical Condition

Are the systems in good operating order, and are the environmental conditions comfortable? Is the system operating economically? What are projected replacment schedules for major equipment? What are the maintenance schedules?

c) State and Local Building Codes

Does the building meet current state and local codes? What are the code implications of renovations or additions? Is the fire alarm system up-to-date? Is the building "fire safe"? Do doors have required closers? Is it "smoke safe"? Does the building meet current standards of accessibility for the handicapped?

d) State Educational Requirements

Does the building meet current requirements for classroom sizes, types, etc.? What are the implications of bringing existing spaces up-to-date if additions or alterations are made to the building? Can the building handle 21st-Century technology requirements? Are classrooms required for special education? Are kindergarten rooms large enough? Is the library big enough to contain the required number of volumes? Is indoor physical education space required? Will the costs of making required changes be excessive in relationship to the existing value of the space?

e) Roof Condition

Is the roof in good condition? Many roofs (especially the flat built-up roofs applied in the late 1960s and early 1970s) have failed or are in the process of failing. The expense incurred in roof repair or replacement is so high it can have a great impact on renovation budgets.

f) Building Size

Is the building properly sized to meet the educational program? Does it have required number and size of spaces (related to state regulations—but also to the goals found in the educational program)? What sizes, types, and configurations are the existing spaces?

g) Aesthetics and Comfort

Is the building attractive and comfortable? Does it meet the aesthetic and quality standards of the educational plan? What does the community think of the building? Does its "image" say "education"? Can it be altered to meet these expectations? Should it?

h) Modification Possibilities

Can the building be renovated or added to economically? Are there "lost spaces" within the building that can be recovered and creatively used for new purposes? The inventory may help discover some out-of-the-way or derelict places which can be architectural and financial boons. Can an addition be avoided by creatively replanning the existing building? Does the condition and value of the building merit an addition?

i) Site and Landscape

Is the site circulation (pedestrian and vehicular) adequate for the current operation of the school? Is it safe? Is it efficient? Is there sufficient parking? Is there parking for the handicapped? Is there a landscape plan? Is current landscape material being maintained? Are the playgrounds or playing fields sufficient? Could new landscape material improve the aesthetic quality of the building or increase energy efficiency?

j) Overall Building Condition

Has the building been properly maintained? Are major capital repairs needed? Is the building worn out? Should the building be torn down? What are the alternatives?

3. *Square Footage Program of Desired Spaces*

Taking into account the goals of the educational program, as well as the special needs for the specific building or group of buildings, a desired square footage program should then be developed. This program should be prepared as an independent part of the study and should not address what exists but instead what is needed. Some factors to be considered while developing the program may include:

a) The spaces needed for learning and teaching the educational program.

b) State guidelines (or requirements) for classroom sizes, library sizes, special classrooms, physical education, etc.

c) State and local codes.

d) Current and projected enrollments.

e) Handicapped accessibility requirements.

Square footages should be developed on a square foot per pupil basis for specific space types using recognized educational space planning guidelines combined with knowledge of local requirements; ergo: 120 square foot/pupil in a high school industrial arts wood shop, or 60 square foot/pupil for an art classroom. These figures are of course influenced by the number of pupil stations required—a smaller than normal number of pupil stations for any given activity will require more square footage per pupil.

Ultimately, the square footage program should include a list of spaces required and their sizes on a per space basis. This list should be subtotaled and multiplied by a percentage factor for circulation, services, and structure. This percentage varies from 25%-45% based on the type of building, type of school, mechanical and electrical requirements, site, special requirements, etc.

4. *Comparison of Existing Space(s) to Desired Square Footage Programs*

On the surface this comparison might seem like simple math, and sometimes it is. In some studies one can take an existing list of spaces and subtract it from a desired square footage program, and the difference will be the size of an addition which is needed. This simple case is usually the exception, however, rather than the rule. Often the comparison is more complex. Existing spaces which are too small, space adjacencies, existing circulation patterns, code problems, and a variety of other circumstances usually cut the efficiency factor of an existing building when it is renovated for new educational uses. These factors should be taken into account when the comparison is done.

In the case of a feasibility study for one specific building, an analysis will need to be made of the existing spaces, their potential alternative uses and how these spaces can serve the new program. Some effort should be made to recover "lost" spaces in the existing building and find ways for them to serve the new program; ergo, basements, attics, old elevator shafts, unused stairways, extra-wide corridors, etc.

When the feasibility study examines a group of buildings, comparisons of existing gross square footage and new desired square footage may point out the need for additions, renovations, or a new building.

5. *Alternatives, Costs, and Schedules*

Square footage comparisons as described in Item 4 above usually generate a number of potential solutions. These alternatives should be looked at as different paths to accomplish desired goals and not as finished architectural solutions. The variables can be presented in diagrammatic form so that areas, general massing and location of spaces/building, etc., can be understood by the client.

Each alternative should be accompanied by sufficient data to enable a desired path to be selected from among the group. Two pieces of information which are usually required are:

a) Construction and project cost estimate.

b) Construction sequence and potential construction schedule.

In the case of a potential building renovation, the owner should know construction schedules and sequences in order to make alternative plans to serve whatever is the existing use of the building. In the case of a group of buildings or a campus plan, these sequences are important for the above reasons as well as for overall capital development planning and fund raising. In the use of a multi-staged project, construction costs will be impacted by project sequencing as well as by potential inflation. All of these factors should be taken into account for each alternative presented.

6. *Summary and Recommendations*

The architect or planner performing the architectural feasibility study should be prepared to recommend to the client a preferred alternative to pursue. This recommendation should take into account the following:

a) Money available.

b) Time available.

c) The political realities.

d) Potential of existing buildings and surrounding land.

The rationale supporting this recommendation should demonstrate that the alternative is logical, flexible, buildable, and will serve the educational program.

In the final judgement, that design which will be best, is the plan which holds most true to the educational goals of the school. The feasibility study should produce architectural diagrams and guidelines which excite our minds both visually and intellectually.

Chapter 2.
Developing The Master Plan

Gaylaird Christopher, AIA*

The master planning starts with a facility survey to determine the enrollment capacity of existing schools. By conducting a survey, the surveyor will look at numerous parameters which affect the functional capacity of a facility. Some of those factors are: building capacities, site size, configuration and topography, and space utilization. The end product of the plan will provide the district, site administrators, district maintenance personnel, and other interested parties with a detailed understanding of facility capacities, needed improvements, and opportunities for future expansion. The plan will determine where space is available, which facilities are overutilized and where additional facilities can be accommodated. Used in conjunction with the district's enrollment projections, the facility master plan should become an integral part of the district's scheduling process. The methodology described herein outlines the step by step process to complete a facilities master plan.

Facility Site Plan

The first critical step in conducting a facility survey is the development of a two-dimensional map of each existing facility. The map, or site plan, should show the entire dimensioned site area, names of surrounding streets, and all critical site features, including buildings, portable classrooms, trailers, parking lots, access roads, and major hardscape areas. Each instructional space on the campus should be identified and separately numbered. All mapping should be done on a 8-1/2 x 11 format to allow for easy reference and reproduction. For larger facilities, e.g. senior high schools, it will be necessary to do two plans: a "Plot Plan of Site and Building" shows the entire site area,

---

*Gaylaird Christopher is a principal with Wolff Long Christopher Architects in Rancho Cucamonga, California.

identifying and numbering major building clusters. The second plan, called "Room Identification Plan" will identify and number each instructional space as discussed above. The actual completion of the drawings should be a fairly simple process. Most districts have available to them record drawings of all existing facilities and additions. These drawings would need to be reduced at the appropriate scale by an architect or professional drafting service. It is critical that the diagrams be accurate and to scale since so many important decisions will be based upon them. Once the drawings are complete, their accuracy should be verified from visual inspection of the site. A legend should be developed to identify symbols used on the site plans. The next step in the process is to gather information about facility utilization and maintenance concerns. The first item in gathering information is to set up a joint meeting with all site administrators for distribution of a "facility questionnaire." At that time, the reasons for the plan should be discussed and the questionnaire explained. It is crucial that the administrators understand the importance of the plan and realize that it will ultimately have a positive effect on their facility. It is also important to make the questionnaire easy to use, flexible, and interesting. If all these conditions are met, it will be used to ensure that the proper information is supplied. Attached to the questionnaire should be a copy of the site plan for that particular school. The site administrator should be directed to make any necessary revisions on the site plan in red and to also show the current room numbering system. It should also show any additional temporary facilities that may have been added since the diagram's completion. Best results are obtained when only a short period of time is allowed for completion of the facility questionnaire. A definite time frame and date should be established for return of the form; normally two weeks is an adequate time frame. It is best if the questionnaires are returned to a district administrator so that they can follow up on any tardy submittals. Once the questionnaires are returned, the surveyor should review each instrument in detail, taking special note of critical factors and unclear information. After the review is completed, an appointment should be made with the site administrator to discuss the questionnaire and to conduct a visual inspection of that facility. The surveyor should carefully review all items which will result in recommending addition to or modification of existing facilities and any items that are unclear. Each room of every school should be visited to verify how it is being utilized. This double checking is essential since facility utilization is so critical in determining enrollment capacity. It is also extremely important that facility utilization is updated on a regular basis so enrollment capacities are reliable. A correction form should also be developed which each site must file with the district administration whenever the classroom use is changed or additions are made. If possible, all schools should be surveyed by the same person to ensure consistency. Once the above information has been compiled, the facility plan can be completed. The facility plan will give the user a concise summary compiling critical information about that particular school.

SCHOOL NUMBER

Schools should be listed alphabetically according to the grade level served:

"E" —designates elementary school
"JH" —designates junior high school
"M" —designates middle school
"H" —designates high school

Development of a district-wide numbering system will establish an easy system for cross-referencing. This is extremely useful for larger districts.

ENROLLMENT HISTORY

School enrollment should be listed for the last five years. The pupils listed should be the official enrollment which is reported to the state on a yearly basis. If an official date has not been defined in the district, then a consistent reporting date should be selected which comes closest to the district-wide peak enrollment for the year.

"SE"—designates special education enrollment

BUILDING AREA

The area of the building should be computed in accordance with your state's criteria. If state criteria are not available, compute as follows:

The architectural area of a building is the sum of the areas of the several floors of the building, including mezzanine and intermediate floored tiers and penthouses of headroom height, measured from the exterior faces of exterior walls or from the centerline of walls separating buildings.

- —Covered walkways, open roofed-over areas that are paved, porches, and similar spaces shall have the architectural area multiplied by an area factor of 0.50.
- —The architectural area does not include such features as pipe trenches, exterior terraces or steps, chimneys, roof over-hangs, etc.

DATES OF CONSTRUCTION

This is the official date when plans are approved by the appropriate jurisdiction.

"Unit(s)" —refers to the building number shown on the site plan.
"OSA No." —refers to the official Office of the State Architect application and approval number. If the State Architect's Office does not have jurisdiction in your area, insert the appropriate agency's name and number.

Dates of construction are extremely important since some states currently have programs to reconstruct buildings over a certain age. If such a program is not available in your area, it is still important to keep track of the age of the buildings as a benchmark for major maintenance, project renovation, reconstruction, or replacement. Most structures require some form of major remodeling or renovation every 25-30 years.

PORTABLES/INADEQUATE AREA

"No./Unit" —the number and type of the portable classroom or unit. The numbers should be run consecutively district-wide.

"P" —designates the portable classroom with a raised wood floor system.

"M" —designates the modular classroom building with a concrete slab or subterranean wood floor system.

"T" —designates a trailer.

The creation of a district-wide numbering and designation system for temporary facilities will improve the district's facility record keeping system in a number of areas. It provides the district a simple way to keep track of the number of portables within the district allowing for easy comparison of permanent versus portable facilities. It also provides a system by which the district can keep track of temporary facilities as they are moved from site to site and provides a record of the facility's age and lease expiration.

DISTRICT POLICY

The district's enrollment recommendations should reflect the district's class size policy according to grade levels served. If the district does not currently have enrollment policies, capacities should be developed based upon what is judged to be educationally prudent for each particular grade level.

STATE CAPACITY STANDARD

The enrollment capacity is based upon the state standards which equals the chargeable building area divided by the appropriate ratio for the grade level served. If the state or district has guidelines for the building area per student, those numbers should be inserted.

If the state doesn't have building area standards, then standards should be assumed so you can evaluate the overall efficiency of each school. Space requirements will vary dramatically depending upon climatic factors and the educational philosophy.

SPACES AND CAPACITY

The spaces and capacity analysis is based upon an actual survey of teaching stations available on each campus. The capacity of any classroom space less than 800 square feet should be reduced. Spaces which are 600 square feet or smaller should not be considered as classrooms.

In older schools where dedicated library space was not designated in the original facility, classrooms which house libraries should not be figured as classrooms.

Enrollment of laboratory or specialized classrooms serving grades 7-12 should be on an adjusted basis for a period day since they cannot be utilized for teaching of subject matters other than those they are designed.

A utilization factor of 90% should be used to adjust capacities of facilities serving grades 7-12 to account for variance in class size and scheduling difficulties. This utilization factor can be adjusted downward based upon past experience.

The classroom capacity criteria should be based upon actual district practices in order to give the most realistic enrollment capacity.

Any assumptions that are made regarding capacity of facilities should be documented as part of the survey in order to allow those who are using the analysis to better understand the criteria and easily modify them in the future.

The spaces and capacity analysis is the most important portion of the facility survey. It is based upon an actual on-site inspection of facilities and their capacities. It will give the user quantitative information which can be used to determine which spaces are available and what facilities will need to be added. It is critical that this analysis be accurate and consistent from site to site. Wherever possible, one person should visit every space within the school district to verify the consistency of the survey. It is also essential for the survey to be updated whenever space utilization changes or facilities are added or deleted.

USABLE PHYSICAL EDUCATION AREA

The usable site area is determined by subtracting unusable site area from gross site area. Unusable area consists of area covered by building, parking lot, area in front of the school and between buildings which is not usable for physical education activities, and sloped areas which are too steep to be used for physical education.

This evaluation requires on-site inspection and development of area calculations based upon the school site plan. The most important function that this review accomplishes is the evaluation of site capacity based upon actual usable area rather than gross land area. This site's specific features, which have a dramatic effect on its ability to accommodate students, are taken into account.

RECOMMENDED SITE CAPACITY

The site capacity is based upon the following ratios of physical education area per student:

Elementary —450 square feet

Junior High — 650 square feet

High School — 500 square feet

These ratios were obtained by protracting recommendations developed by the California Department of Education. If the local factors and/or physical education program demand that more or less area be provided, ratios should be adjusted.

POSSIBLE EXPANSION

This analysis will help the district identify the number of classrooms and accordingly students that can be feasibly added to each campus. The expansion recommendations should be based upon the usable physical education area, existing enrollment levels, and district capacity policy. Tentative location of future temporary facilities should be selected and mapped. Determining a tentative location will hopefully avoid haphazard last minute placement of temporary facilities.

MAXIMUM CAPACITY

The maximum capacity is determined by adding the additional students developed from the "Possible Expansion" analysis to the spaces and capacity recommendation.

Chapter 3.

Writing Educational Specifications

*John H. Fredrickson**

Planning, designing, and building schools destined to be used well into the 21st Century is an awesome responsibility. To provide school facilities which are durable, functional, adaptable, and, at the same time, economical, is a challenge for America's school planners. The reaction of many educators to this challenge has been encouraging. They are re-examining every facet of the teaching-learning process in an attempt to obtain greater efficiency and productivity. The curriculum has been under almost constant review. Basic philosophies regarding such things as the length of the school day and year and traditional teaching and grading methods have also been carefully re-evaluated. The old order is changing, and with this change educators are beginning to recognize the need for more flexible kinds of school structures which will be more hospitable to the educational programs and practices of the future.

Good school facilities are based on good planning, imaginative designing, and modern building. However, even imaginative designs and modern construction methods cannot produce truly effective school facilities without thorough planning. Such planning must be the result of cooperative efforts on the parts of school board members, administrators, teachers, non-professional staff, and outside educational consultants. These cooperative efforts will culminate in the development of educational specifications or program requirements from which a school architect creates preliminary drawings and makes construction cost estimates.

Perhaps the least understood words in educational circles today are the words "educational specifications." Few educators and fewer lay persons

---

*John H. Fredrickson is an educational consultant based in Merrimac, Wisconsin.

understand their meaning with respect to the construction of new school facilities or the renovation of older structures. Until quite recently, the practice of actually writing detailed educational specifications for either new construction or renovation was unheard of in far too many school districts throughout the country. School officials who discussed their curricular plans with an outside educational consultant were rare. Getting educators to think in terms of long-range planning strategies was more rare. Even today, while school planning procedures appear to be improving, there is still much need for upgrading. Given the above, the purpose here will be to present some guidelines for educators charged with the responsibility of developing effective educational specifications.

To begin, a school planning team, consisting of representatives of the administration, teachers, non-professional personnel, and outside consultants should be assembled. As good school plant planning demands, the participation of all groups directly involved in the educational enterprise, the school planning team, is an imperative and its membership should be carefully recruited. The task of the team will be to prepare in-depth background studies in four problem areas before writing the educational specifications or program requirements for a specific project. These problem areas are:

—*educational philosophy and objectives* (all governing policies should be re-examined periodically to insure their continuing validity and to determine whether they have been properly implemented in the past);

—*present educational programs and practices* (any plan for educational improvement must involve a thorough review of present activities);

—*current educational trends and innovations* (motivation for educational change is most often generated by outside forces);

—*educational expectations of the school community* (no plans for change can afford to ignore the general public).

Utilizing the information gathered during the above investigations, the school planning team should then direct its attention to developing the educational specifications under the following categories:

STATEMENT OF PHILOSOPHY

Every school district should have its own educational philosophy as part of the established board policies. If this is not the case, here is an excellent opportunity for the school planning team, representing the board of education, administration, teachers, and non-professional personnel, to develop a philosophy both for the district and the particular school project under consideration.

Hopefully, every educational philosophy would contain a statement relative to fostering a respect for our democratic society through education. It might state that education should help each student to acquire ideas, information, understanding, and skills enabling him or her to get along with others and thus helping to lay the foundations for social responsibility. And finally, the philosophy might point out that education should teach every student that people live, work, think, and speak in a variety of acceptable ways.

GRADE LEVEL TO BE ACCOMMODATED

This portion of the educational specifications should indicate either the actual grades to be included in the new or renovated facilities or the ages of the young people to be enrolled. Here note that possibly a school facility originally designated as an elementary building might at a later date be expected to serve as a middle school. Such planning could very well preclude the necessity of major structural modifications in the future.

ENROLLMENT CAPACITY EXPECTATIONS

Every school district ought to have an ongoing enrollment projection program. The most widely accepted is the so-called survival ratio technique. The first step in this procedure is to estimate future enrollments by computing the possible size of each grade for the next immediate year from the size of the current year's next lower grade. Of the youngsters in any given grade, a certain percentage "survives" to enter the next higher grade the following year. This percentage may be more or less than 100 percent depending primarily on population changes but also somewhat on the promotional policies of the particular school or district.

By computing an average of what this percentage of grade to grade survival has been for the past five to ten years, it becomes possible to advance the current total enrollment year by year, each time dropping the last year and adding a new first grade or kindergarten. Data on pre-school children can also be incorporated in the survival ratio technique.

Using the enrollment projection information, the school planning team will then be required to consider the various methods of grouping students (large and small group instruction, independent study and research, and individual counseling), and to arrive at some judgments concerning the best type of floor plan: open (no interior load-bearing walls); planned variability (some interior load-bearing walls); or standard "eggcrate" (all interior load-bearing walls).

CURRICULAR PROGRAMS AND ACTIVITIES

Among the many factors which have been instrumental in changing and broadening curriculum have been the changing theories about learning. These include the older faculty psychology with its emphasis on mental discipline through formal exercises which was a serious obstacle to curricular improvement and the more modern psychology with its emphasis on the learner that has begun to exert a powerful influence for real progress in education.

Today's definition of curriculum has come to include not only the multitude of school subjects now being offered but all student activities and experiences which are school-directed. With the acceptance of this definition of the curriculum, schools now have many new responsibilities and problems. It must be decided how new courses are to be offered—through insertion in existing subject-matter instruction, through combination, through individualizing of subjects, or through supervised self-study or correspondence study. Consideration must also be given to the new extra-curricular activities, many of which are now carried on after normal school hours. The problem for today and tomorrow is to develop a curriculum for all youth with educational opportunities and services suited to their individual needs and yet sufficient for the successful continuation of democratic society.

With the above firmly in mind, the school planning team must now determine exactly what subjects will be offered and what related activities will take place in the new or renovated facilities. The designation of the intended structure as an elementary, middle, junior, or senior high school will be the major factor. In any event, the groundwork suggested earlier, dealing with the district's present educational programs and activities, current educational trends and innovations, and educational expectations of the school community, will prove to be invaluable in preparing this part of the educational specifications.

SPECIFIC UTILIZATION PLAN

The overall use of the proposed facilities is the topic of this section. Many school districts are considering the utilization of school buildings for year-round instruction, evening community programs, and all kinds of indoor and outdoor recreational activities. Therefore, serious emphasis should be given to such things as air-conditioning, adult meeting facilities, handicapped requirements, and convenient outdoor access ways to various parts of the building for after school use.

INSTRUCTIONAL PROCEDURES

Wide spread innovation in education is still far from a ground swell shaking the nation. Of all the new ideas in education today, only curriculum modification has made any significant inroads in America's schools generally. All of the other ideas for educational improvement, such as closed circuit television, computer-assisted and computer-managed instruction, modular scheduling, advanced placement, and nongrading, have not touched more than fifteen percent of the school districts in the country. Even a time-tested procedure like teaming has not been extensively adopted in America's schools!

The school planning team, employing the information it gathered during the groundwork phase dealing with current educational trends and innovations, should now attempt to relate these findings to the curricular program and activities determined earlier.

TEACHING SPACE REQUIREMENTS

Not all subjects and activities require the same amount of space and facilities to be effectively accomplished. Therefore, the school planning team should review its deliberations of the new instructional procedures just considered and its recent decisions on the curricular program and activities to find the optimum space requirements, equipment, and specific location for each teaching category. Teacher expertise should be fully utilized during the work on this section.

SPECIALIZED INSTRUCTIONAL FACILITIES

In this matter, the school planning team concerns itself with the listing, defining, and describing of the special instructional areas other than classroom or teaching station space. Here such things as the library or instructional materials center, auditorium, gymnasium, shops, computer rooms, special education facilities, music and art rooms, and the so-called multi-purpose room should be considered in great detail. Once again, the teaching staff members of the school planning team directly involved with these kinds of special facilities should be strongly encouraged to exercise their respective expertise.

AUXILIARY AREAS OR FACILITIES

Auxiliary areas are often referred to as housekeeping facilities. In this case the school planning team must be concerned about the location and adequacy of office space, faculty, health, speech, and special conference rooms, food service, custodial and storage areas, restrooms, and outdoor play and parking facilities. Considerable time and thought should be given to these vital services to insure functional operation of the entire new or renovated school building.

MISCELLANEOUS CONCERNS

This section of the educational specifications can be extremely useful in handling matters not covered fully under other categories (such as clock and bell systems, intercommunications, telephones, television outlets, fire alarms, incineration facilities, etc.) or as a vehicle to advise or instruct the architect on concerns not previously considered (such as the acoustical, illuminational, thermal, and visual environmental requirements). Expensive "change orders" after construction or renovation has actually begun can often be precluded if this section is thoughtfully developed by the school planning team.

CLOSING OR SUMMARY STATEMENT

This final section is, unfortunately, often omitted by school planning teams. It is here that the educational philosophy developed for the school building or district, reinforced by all of the data and information of the earlier sections, should be restated for the convenience of the architect. Any requirements that the team feels to be imperative should be noted as well as those which are open to team-architect negotiation later.

When the educational specifications have finally been developed and reasonable consensus reached on their merits, the next step is the selection of a school architect. A number of architectural firms should be invited to interview. They should be required to present photographs, floor plans, and total construction cost data for school construction and renovation projects they have designed and built in the recent past. They should welcome direct inquiry with other school planning teams relative to their overall cooperation and successful completion of modern school building projects.

School planning teams ought to make a point of visiting those schools both to inspect and to ask questions using their own newly developed educational specifications as a working guide.

CONCLUSIONS

When the school district takes the time, money, and effort to commission a dedicated school planning team assisted by outside educational consultants and that combination develops realistic educational specifications and selects a competent school architect, it can be assured that the new or renovated school building will indeed function effectively well into the 21st Century.

Chapter 4.
Selection of An Architect

Wallace Underwood[*]

The selection of an architect is the most important part of any building project. An architect should be selected who is willing to build the building the school district wants, not what the architect wants. The ideal architect is one whose thinking is akin to that of the school administrator and staff who will administer, teach students, and maintain the building after completion.

INVITED PROPOSALS

The district should invite proposals from architects. A pre-qualification questionnaire should be developed by the school district asking the architect questions that are of interest to the district and valuable in the selection process; it should include the following areas:

1. *The Firm*
   a. Where is the firm located?
      The school district may want to establish a maximum distance from the school district that the firm must be located in order to be considered for the project. This could affect the architect's accessibility and service.

   b. How many years has the firm been doing business?

   c. What is the firm's experience in designing public school buildings? How many school buildings has the firm designed?

   d. How many staff members in the firm? Architects ____, Engineers ____, Specialists ____.

---

[*]Wallace Underwood is Superintendent, School Town of Munster, Munster, Indiana.

      e. Where are your plans prepared?

      f. Does your firm provide consultants? What kind?

2. *Firm's Experience*
   a. What is your experience in designing energy efficient and maintenance free buildings?

   b. Will you provide energy cost analysis? Is there an extra charge for this service?

   c. How do you handle change orders?

3. *Architect's Mistakes*
   a. Who pays for the architect's mistakes and/or omissions?

4. *General Information*
   a. What are your current project commitments?

   b. How long does it take after preliminary drawings are accepted by the Board to prepare final drawings and specifications?

5. *Legal Action*
   a. Has a school district ever brought legal action against your firm? If so, please explain.

   b. Have you ever brought legal action against a school district? If so, please explain.

   c. Have you ever been involved in legal action with a contractor concerning a school project? If so, please explain.

6. *Fees and Services*
   a. How do you determine your fee for new construction and remodeling?

   b. What services does this firm provide for this fee?

   c. How much supervision will be provided? The district may be required to pay an additional amount if they want more supervision than the architect is willing to provide in this basic fee.

   d. Would you be willing to participate and assist in site selection?

After proposals and questionnaires have been received from architects, they should be reviewed by the administrative staff. The number of architects should be reduced to a manageable number. Three to five would be ideal. The administration and board should make inspections of the projects that the architects have completed that are of a similar nature to the district's project, i.e., new elementary school, new middle school, new high school, or major renovation of an elementary school, middle school, or high school.

After inspection of the architects' projects, a rating sheet should be developed for board members to rate the architects. From this rating the board should decide whether it wishes to continue investigating an architect or would want to drop the firm from consideration.

Interviews should be set up with the board and the architects. Interviews should be a give and take proposition with the architect given at least one hour total. The hour should consist of 20 minutes for the architect to make a presentation and 40 minutes for questions and answers. Time should be allowed after each interview for the board to have a brief discussion concerning the architect previously interviewed. The architectural interviews should be scheduled at least fifteen minutes apart; three interviews in one evening should be the maximum. Each board member should be given an evaluation sheet for each architect. After all architects have been interviewed, the board should then rate the architects individually and narrow the choice down to no more than two. A discussion on those two architects should be of sufficient length for the board to reach a consensus that those are the architects under final consideration. At this point the board may wish to invite the finalists back for another interview and visit their offices and additional projects completed by the architects. Previous clients should be contacted to determine their satisfaction with the architects.

After the board has reached a decision on the architect, the one major thing left to be accomplished is the development of the contract with the architect.

ARCHITECT'S CONTRACT

The standard AIA Contract is a beginning point, and it should be negotiable. Architectural fees can vary substantially on new buildings and/or remodeling. The fee schedule should be clearly understood and written into the contract prior to the final selection or ratification of the contract. If several projects are contemplated over a period of years, perhaps a contract could be agreed upon on a volume basis. Architectural work completed within so many years would all be done at a substantially lower rate. Roofing projects should carry a lower fee schedule than other types of architectural work as they require less work on the part of the architect.

Often there is a misunderstanding on the amount of supervision that is to be provided by the architect. This should be clearly agreed upon and written into the contract. If the school board expects the architect to be present five days a week, four days a week, or three days a week, this should be clearly stated in the contract. Obviously there are times when it may not be necessary for the architect to be present during a project, i.e., when there is not much work taking place. However, misunderstandings do occur if it is not clearly spelled out in the architect's contract.

ARCHITECT'S COORDINATOR

There should be a clear understanding and agreement by the board as to who will be coordinating the project for the architect. This person should also be interviewed by the board and administration.

In conclusion, the architect, the citizens and the professionals in a school district should have a sound basis for a solid relationship. Preparation is the foundation for success.

SUMMARY

Educational facility needs and fiscal responsibility are ultimately addressed by the Board of Education. Many thousands and possibly millions of dollars could be saved each year in building educational facilities if the appropriate steps were taken in the selection of the architect. To do this the board should establish a selection process which includes a clear view of the policy used in the selection process. A sample policy which gives stability to the selection process includes equitable guidelines in working with many architects. Once the board determines these for their particular needs then it is systematic to have a clear understanding of the flow of selection procedures. This is the "nuts and bolts" approach to an objective selection. The flow may differ from board to board, but the need for a smooth flow of procedures is great enough for a plan to be determined and followed. The board has many responsibilities, but to re-invent the wheel is not one of them. A way to avoid this is to try the suggestions given herein.

Chapter 5.
School Site Selection

*Ken Falkinham**

During the past decade, school administrators have had few opportunities to construct new facilities or buildings or for that matter to purchase appropriate school sites for future use. With declining enrollments, districts were facing the issue of closing schools and/or attempting to sell surplus land which was perceived in the 1960s or 1970s to be needed. Facility and site selection is, however, still a pertinent topic for discussion, especially in high growth areas around the country.

The farsighted school board and administration will project their school site needs well into the future and acquire adequate sites while land is still available and relatively economical. In selecting a school site, the following basic criteria should be considered:

1. Economic, social, and housing makeup of the community.
2. Integration with community planning and zoning.
3. Relationship of high schools and/or elementary schools to other governmental districts such as township, county, or city.
4. Site location, i.e., urban, suburban, rural and usability of site for building, recreation, etc., as it pertains to water table, flood plain, subsoil conditions.
5. Utility services as related to availability and costs. Are gas, electricity, sewer and water utilities near? Are initial costs of land versus cost of improvements satisfactory?

The site selection process should be initiated by a team of experts composed of school administrative officials, an architect, and educational consultants. These core individuals would also probably require assistance of landscape architects, regional planners, engineers/recreational experts, and legal consultants. The team members should have a thorough understanding

---

* *Ken Falkinham is Director of Fiscal Affairs, Township High School District #113, Highland Park, Illinois.*

of the district's programs and/or educational specifications. The team should make a recommendation to the board of education answering the following questions in detail:
1. Where should the site be?
2. How large should the site be?
3. What specific characteristics should the site possess?
4. What cost is reasonable for the site?

The site selection team members can usually make specific contributions in arriving at the ultimate site selected. The contributions are mentioned below. This list is not all inclusive and a district may wish to "customize" its team to meet its specific needs.

SCHOOL ADMINISTRATION

The school district's administration can share with the team members the educational needs of the district and just what is required in terms of space and curriculum needs.

ARCHITECT

The architect can project the site characteristics that best accommodate the building design suggested by the district's educational specification. Preliminary sketches on proposed sites can be helpful in recognizing both good and undesirable site features.

LANDSCAPE ARCHITECT

This architect can assist in placing the building on proposed sites which would allow optimum development of the total area and can provide information concerning topography, soil conditions, drainage, etc. Also, once the site has been selected he/she can assist in development of walks, play fields, appropriate plantings and outdoor learning areas.

ENGINEERS

Soil consultants or engineers are a critical part of the site selection team. Laboratory analyses of soils to determine conditions needed for proper bearing of the structure and proper drainage of the surface water are vital. The worst thing that could happen to a district would be to purchase a site that has an unbuildable subsurface.

REAL ESTATE APPRAISER

This person can conduct a study to assist the team in obtaining a reasonable price for the site selected. The person is especially important if the district must initiate condemnation proceedings with its right of eminent domain.

LEGAL CONSULTANT

This key person provides legal advice to the board of education by examining all legal documents pertaining to the purchase of property or condemnation proceedings.

URBAN AND REGIONAL PLANNERS

The planner can assist in analyzing and mapping areas to help locate school sites. This person can also advise on zoning regulations and proposed highway construction. The ideal parcel of land to be selected by the team for recommendation to the board of education should survive the selection process by meeting at least two-thirds of the criteria listed below:

—Will the site support the educational program?
—Is the site's location convenient for the majority of the pupils?
—Is the site the right size and shape?
—Is the topography conducive to desired site development?
—Is the site safe?
—Is the site free of industrial and traffic noise?
—Does the site drain properly and are the soil conditions good?
—Is water, gas, and electricity available?
—Is the site served by police and fire departments?
—Is the site expandable in the future?
—Is the price affordable?
—Is the site available?

SITE DEVELOPMENT PLAN

Once the team has accumulated all pertinent information on all sites being considered, it is possible to begin developing a land-use plan which details possible solutions, in a preliminary manner, of land engineering concerns such as grades and placement of parking areas, roads and walkways, landscape design, and a plan of outdoor learning and athletic areas. The following steps may be helpful for the team as they approach this phase of site selection.

Step 1 Obtain a topographical survey of the site. These maps may be obtained from the U.S. Coast and Geodetic Survey or from the State Highway Department.

Step 2 Have the team make repeated visits to all sites to gain a feeling for the character of the sites, to collect information, and to begin a land-use analysis. The architect will usually mark down pertinent information which might influence site selection. The team makes these studies so they can visualize the site as it will be at completion of the developed school.

Step 3 The architect should develop freehand sketches expressing the educational specifications of the board of education on hard-line drawings. Collaboration with school planners, landscape architects, engineers, and other experts will, through free interchange of ideas, allow for the best plan concept to evolve for each site. With these sketches in hand, the team should be better able to visualize the site possibilities and strengths versus its shortcomings.

Additional Criteria To Be Considered

SIZE OF SITE

The size of a school site should be determined largely by the nature and scope of the contemplated educational program. Numerous state authorities have developed recommendations for site size. These authorities conclude the following:

ELEMENTARY SCHOOLS

Suggested size is ten (10) acres plus one (1) additional acre for each one hundred (100) pupils in the projected ultimate maximum enrollment. An elementary school of 450 pupils should have an acreage of approximately 14.50 acres.

MIDDLE SCHOOLS

Suggested size is twenty (20) acres plus one (1) additional acre for each 100 pupils. Thus a site of minimum size for a middle school of five hundred (500) pupils would be 25 acres.

HIGH SCHOOLS

For senior high schools it is suggested that there be provided a minimum site of thirty (30) acres plus an additional acre for each one hundred (100) pupils. Thus a site for a senior high school of 1,000 pupils would be 40 acres.

COST

A board of education must be extremely careful in considering the cost of a site. A site that may seem high in initial cost may be most economical in the long run. Conversely, an inexpensive piece of property may be expensive to develop. A complete set of construction estimates should be made on all sites to weight the *total* cost of a site purchase and development.

PEDESTRIAN AND VEHICLE TRAFFIC

A site viewed in an undeveloped state must be looked at with great vision. The traffic patterns for both motor vehicles and pedestrians should be analyzed as to the impact on safety and efficient and timely transportation of students and staff. The number and type of entry roads near the site and the number and types of vehicles utilizing the roads should be looked at. The number of parking spaces versus the available land should be reviewed. The most accepted rule of thumb on the number of parking spaces needed is:

School	Parking Spaces
Elementary	One per classroom + 3
Junior High	One per classroom + 6
High School	One per classroom + 11

Separate parking areas for staff versus student and visitor parking is desirable. Also, all parking and curbing should provide for handicap accessibility.

COMPARING ALTERNATIVE SITES

When a board of education has more than one (1) site to choose from, a criteria evaluation should be set up to objectively evaluate all sites. Architects and administrators have developed over the years numerous scales—some extensive, some not too elaborate. The evaluation form shown below directs a selection of a site which would not be the cheapest in initial cost but the most desirable incorporating the ten (10) categories listed.

COMPARING ALTERNATE SITES

Each factor weighted on scale of 1 to 10, for desirability	SITE A	SITE B	SITE C	SITE D
Program support	7	7	5	10
Ease of acquisition	9	10	4	6
Cost of site development	10	6	6	9
Cost of utilities	3	5	7	10
Aesthetic quality	10	9	4	7
Location and centrality to pupil population	3	6	8	9
Ease of future expansion	5	7	4	2
Future land value and marketability	4	6	6	10
Adaptability to future grade organization changes	7	7	7	8
Cost	5	8	4	6
Total evaluation	63	71	55	77

To conclude—a selection of a school site can be the start of a truly rewarding experience for any administrator. It can also be a traumatic occurrence as the "experts" on the sideline continue to second guess the selection team's choice. If the leadership of the site selection team diligently does his/her job, the process should be completed smoothly. If the team does its job, the old axiom below may prove inappropriate.

I know of no matter of taste in which so remarkable a similarity prevails throughout our state as in the selection of the site for a school-house. The side line of the public highway and the most worthless parcel of land in the district, if the two can be found in juxtaposition, seem to be the favored locality. (from THE SECOND REPORT OF THE BOARD OF EDUCATION OF THE STATE OF MAINE, 1848)

Chapter 6.
Spaces for Learning

*Timothy Brown**

It used to be from the cynics that one heard, "What goes around, comes around ... education is always in the state of swinging from one end of the instructional pendulum to the other." However, one need not study too much history of education, nor teach too many years to be impressed with the validity of this seemingly flippant remark. To be sure, each extreme swing brings with it a new body of research, a new set of experts, and a new list of titles, but basic outcomes ring frighteningly familiar.

The sixties brought us J. Lloyd Trump and Delmas F. Miller as the spokespersons for a drastic new approach to teaching and learning. Espousing the belief that learners respond in varying ways to instructional techniques, the NASSP-sponsored Model Schools Project promoted independent study, differentiated staffing, small group interaction, large group lecture, flexible-modular scheduling, team-teaching, and teacher advisement as the way to deliver this philosophy.

Then came the "back to basics" purge of the seventies calling for a rise in test scores, more emphasis on student discipline and renewed attention to career and vocational education. The individual gave way to the group and the lecture-discussion, albeit more lecture than discussion, again became the dominant, virtually exclusive, mode of instruction. However, the seventies have quickly slipped into the eighties and are beginning to bear striking similarities to the sixties.

Do not worry, the Model School Project is dead ... Flexible-modular scheduling has not been resuscitated ... Students are still under control ... However, the literature on hemisphericity and brain dominance, which has begotten the 4-MAT system of teaching and learning, bears striking resemblance to the individualized instructional programs of the Model Schools,

---

*Timothy Brown is Principal, Andrew High School, Tinley Park, Illinois.

Westinghouse PLAN and others. The current literature on critical thinking unashamedly uses the same hierarchies of cognitive, affective and psychomotor domains that were so integral to the individualized programs of twenty years ago. As a crowning example, the most recent ASCD video tape series on thinking skills promotes a middle school program where young thinkers sit around in lounge chairs sharing great thoughts with their teacher and each other. Deja vu?

Such concepts as interdisciplinary team teaching, pontoon scheduling, and teacher advisement, so much a part of the earlier, individualized instruction formats, are once again finding their way into those schools on the cutting edge of quality instruction in the eighties. While the research supporting these programs is not all new, a revived interest in the individual and his/her need for a broad base of academic and social experiences has caused educators to rethink some of the philosophies that seemed to temporarily fall into disfavor.

While the purpose of this document is not to present an anecdotal history of education from 1960 to the present, nor to juxtapose the social condition of the country with the dominant instructional techniques in schools, it would be foolish to assume that these phenomena do not impact school buildings. Scores of buildings were built in the late sixties to be "Model Schools" high schools. Boasting an abundance of open space, theater-like lecture halls, tiny discussion rooms, and centralized media centers, these buildings were expected to facilitate, even guarantee, the individualization of instruction. As these buildings were being built, teachers who would be staffing them were being indoctrinated in the rudiments of individualized instruction. Dozens of consultants earned a handsome living with their dog and pony shows espousing the philosophy and training the techniques of individualization of instruction. From teaching-learning units, with their carefully delineated behaviorally stated objectives, to the techniques of small group interaction, the newly trained teacher was expected to completely shed the old way of teaching and learning and embrace individualization as his/her own. For all kinds of reasons it did not work . . .

Was it that teachers were not properly trained? Were students too immature to handle the lack of social structure? Were parents unwilling to accept a mode of teaching and learning drastically unlike their own? Were teachers too entrenched in teaching the way they were taught to make such a major change? Probably, the answer is "all of the above." However, what about those buildings?

The tragic reality was that the beautiful new "Model Schools" buildings were grossly unfit for traditional instruction. Thirty students could not adequately fit into a seminar room designed for eight. Four teachers could not lecture simultaneously in the same open space. A class of thirty did not need a lecture hall built for two hundred. A large student commons was not necessary for a tightly scheduled school day. In short, a philosophy too quickly tested gave way to community heartache and personal tragedy in the name of what seemed best for kids. Beautiful edifices were carved into instructional nightmares as the pendulum so quickly changed its course. Architects, superintendents, principals, and school boards found themselves looking for work as the newly enlightened found their way into power. A hurtful marriage of philosophy and practice had come to awkward dissolution.

However, the philosophy was not totally ill-founded. The techniques of "Model Schools" were not without merit. As contemporary literature reaffirms, probably more quality instructional theory was made real during the sixties than most would be willing to acknowledge. However, the sixties represented a trendy pendulum extreme, and were therefore doomed to failure.

So, what made the individualized instruction programs of the sixties trendy extremes, when the research of the eighties supports many of the same constructs, albeit tempered and modified?

Clearly, it was the buildings.

School districts in the market for new high school buildings were lured by the philosophy of individualized instruction and the economy of open space. With little attention to instructional methodology, and less sensitivity to the complex issues of teacher training, dozens of buildings were made in the image and likeness of "Model Schools" schools. However, these buildings proved quickly not to be the guarantors of individualized instruction. Rather they served to guarantee the demise of the same. By launching into buildings before the instruction was in place, the training of staff took a backseat to the demands of bricks and mortar. By implementing a flexible schedule before the curriculum demanded flexibility, student control and lack of social structure became the target of public attention. The so-called open space flexible high school became a symbol of inflexibility. By forcing a philosophy on a poorly prepared professional staff, these buildings degraded and insulated the professionalism of the very people they were expected to convert.

While some architects would have professional educators believe that they know what is best for teaching and learning, it is time to reverse this demeaning trend. A philosophy of instruction will only survive if the professionals responsible for delivering it are committed to its tenets and trained in its practice. Professional educators, not architects and consultants, must be calling the shots on appropriate space for teaching and learning. Buildings must not be built to convert a staff to a newly agreed upon agenda. Buildings should not be called upon to carry the burden of effective teacher training and continual supervision of instruction.

Therefore, the most important resources in designing a school building are the professional staff members who will be practicing there. Qualified educators, accustomed to practicing their highly sophisticated profession, are singularly suited to the designing of quality instructional space. In this manner, the practiced philosophy will dictate the requirements of the building rather than vice versa. The building will not be designed until a well-trained group of practicing educators gives its approval to the space that will become its own. However, this does not address the potential for a philosophy change, the improvement of instruction, and the all-too-familiar pendulum swing.

The trendy pendulum swings of the sixties and the concomitant reaction of the seventies were clearly exacerbated by the construction of trendy buildings. No community can afford to allow the trendy, albeit well intentioned, philosophy of a select few to override the common practice of a respected majority. While some of the most valid components of the individualized instruction were thrown out in a knee jerk reaction to the buildings in which they were housed, many of those components proved to be impervious to their housing and are successfully practiced in quality schools everywhere. Independent study has been well accepted as a method of challenging the best and brightest of secondary school students. Small group interaction is recognized as a vital component in hundreds of discussion-oriented classrooms. Team teaching is successfully practiced in schools designed to meet the needs of a wide variety of academic and curriculum needs. Teacher advisement programs are currently serving as the backbone of many high quality secondary school programs. Moreover, not one of these techniques requires classroom space so unique that it excludes others.

By careful analysis then, one may well hypothesize that the pendulum swings in quality instruction are not all that drastic. If successful practices of the sixties can be equally successful in the eighties, it can be assumed that professional educators are more concerned with what works than with what they are being told to do. It can be acknowledged that practicing educators are not so willing to grasp at extremes as they are willing to pick and choose from a variety of thoughtfully presented options.

For this reason, those responsible for designing and building quality instruction should not be disillusioned by the trends they plot, the books they read, and the consultants they employ. Rather, they must give thoughtful ear to those who will most intimately be using the space they are about to prepare. Indeed traditional has become far more flexible than the flexible design of the late sixties.

In summary, it is essential that those charged with the responsibility for creating instructional space do not count on resource books and educational consultants to tell them what to build. Practicing educational consultants are keenly aware of the research and pedagogy of effective teaching. They know first hand about what works and what has proved impractical. They speak eloquently about what techniques they have accepted as their own and what have proved ineffectual. They know their students and what it takes, both physically and psychologically, to allow them to learn. The trendy construction of times past served to insult and demean the most important dimension in a quality learning environment—the professional educator. Let that mistake never be made again.

Chapter 7.
Building Interiors

*Dawn R. Day**

It's a matter of style, function ... and quality. These are the characteristics that a discerning individual or school system searches for in the creation of an interior environment.

STYLE

From inspiring classroom spaces to functional multi-purpose spaces, from exciting student commons to athletic facilities, the interiors should reflect the type of people who use them. Successful interiors are responsive to people and to architecture, but they achieve a certain character and originality all their own. Because they evoke a strong and immediate response from people, interior environments must be carefully structured to reinforce a school's particular image and provide a harmonious atmosphere for a complete range of activities by students, faculty, and patrons. Thus, the creation of interior space is a significant but delicate task.

FUNCTION

Interior design, of course, goes far beyond selecting furnishings, colors, and finishes. Design is a problem-solving art requiring technical as well as artistic ability, demanding a thorough understanding of today's rapidly changing technology, and a recognition of the impact of that technology on tomorrow's schools. Ultimately, each interior space must serve the purpose for which it was created. Sufficient time and effort should be spent researching, evaluating, and documenting each area's needs within the school. Special consideration must be given to adjacency requirements, flexibility, circulation patterns, special area needs, growth, and the overall efficiency of space while enhancing the activities of students and faculty who will use the environment. In the end, even the most eye-catching interior must respond to the user's functional needs to be successful.

---

*Dawn R. Day is an Interior Designer with Thompson, Ventulett and Stainback Architects, Atlanta, Georgia.

QUALITY

It shows in the finished product. It is imperative to select a designer who is an experienced professional, dedicated to quality design, and knowledgeable about education who understands the importance of creating interiors on time and within budget. The designer should be knowledgeable enough to recommend and use additional consultants, as needed, to produce a design that is responsive to the area, is functional, and is of high quality.

Spaces For Learning

Instructional spaces are all too frequently taken for granted by those who plan educational facilities as well as those who use them. Designers and planners lack adequate criteria of classroom efficiency; instructors and students tend to adopt a fatalistic attitude toward educational facilities. There is agreement that a school's physical plant should mirror its educational philosophy, but the methods for achieving this are elusive. The present rectangular room with its straight rows of chairs and wide windows was intended to provide for ventilation, light, quick departure, ease of supervision, and a host of other legitimate needs as they existed in the early 1900s. That was a century ago, and despite new developments in lighting, acoustics, temperature control, equipment, and construction, most school buildings are still boxes filled with cubes containing a specified number of chairs in straight rows. There have been attempts to break away from this rigid pattern, but change comes slowly to education.

It is clear that teachers must learn how to use instructional spaces and facilities. However, one cannot introduce change in the teaching environment without discussing new program possibilities with the instructional staff, pupils, and parents. Otherwise, it is likely that people will continue to do what they have always done even though a greater range of activities are possible. They will do less well because the new environment is designed for other sorts of activities.

There are many assumptions about student seating. Many teachers will say that the front rows contain the most interested students, those in the rear engage in illicit activities, students at the aisles are mainly concerned with the quick departures, most absentees come from the rear quadrant farthest from the windows, and that desks arranged in straight rows inhibit discussion. If shoulder to shoulder seating discourages communication in an "old-folks" home, what does it do to a student's attitude toward school and the teacher's attitude toward students? Is it degrading to sit shoulder to shoulder with strangers front and back, to be so close together that knees touch, where privacy is impossible? All this should make educators wonder about the connection between the classroom layout and student participation.

The Acoustical Environment

One of the physical factors related to the design of a facility has to do with the acoustical environment. Good sound conditions are necessary so that students and teachers can communicate. If the classroom situation does not offer a good listening environment, the educational process cannot function at peak efficiency. Recent research on the effect of sound on the learning process has shed new light on the reaction of students to the presence of disturbing noise levels. According to some studies, in order to tune out the noise, the student also tunes out the instruction.

It goes without saying that good hearing conditions are important. The ear is an extremely adaptive organ, capable of detecting recognizable phrases out of a babble of sounds. Human energy is expended in the process of hearing with the amount being relative to how good or bad the sound conditions may be. The ear ranks second only to the eye as a corridor to the mind; therefore, the acoustical environment of the school assumes cardinal importance in the learning situation. Physiological effects such as nausea, fatigue, headache, and loss of muscular coordination have been directly related to certain noises as documented by numerous studies. The major effects of unwanted sound on students are an annoyance, loss of efficiency, auditory fatigue and partial or permanent hearing loss.

A room should have comparatively even proportions in depth and width rather than extreme dimension in either direction. This configuration proves beneficial for both sight and sound. Rooms with floor and wall surfaces of slightly irregular planes will generally have better acoustical qualities than standard box shaped rooms. Sound should be directed toward the audience. The use of soft floor, wall, and window coverings influences sound control both from impact noise and other distracting sounds. Students like warm, comfortable floors, and both students and teachers alike feel that behavior problems are reduced when carpet is used.

Acoustical treatment should be computed on a room by room basis depending upon its use, size, and shape. Educators should insist that competent acoustical consultants participate in planning a school in the same manner as the structural, lighting, heating, or kitchen consultants are used. Properly utilized acoustical materials can produce a profound effect throughout any building. Techniques can include pan-type concrete construction, treatment of the upper wall sections of high areas rather than ceilings, use of acoustical panels, patches, and strips. Hanging banners are not only attractive but also help with sound absorption.

The Visual Environment

The human eye is perhaps the most versatile of all human organs, yet this versatility saps our energy. Under normal circumstances, the human eye consumes one-fourth of the total body energy. The eyes can pass on many problems to other body organs without our being aware of it. Overtaxed eyes may create headaches, nausea, dizziness, loss of appetite, vomiting, and complete physical exhaustion; but few are aware of what is causing the problem.

Approximately 80 percent of all learning is acquired through vision. Therefore, proper lighting and color are necessary for proper optical hygiene. The visual environment is a much broader concept than just lighting; therefore, educational planners and designers must be concerned with natural and artificial lighting, brightness differences, reflection coefficients, and interior decoration. Every instructional area in the educational facility should possess an environment that promotes the visual health of its occupants.

LIGHTING

Historically, there has been no optimum value of light intensity recommended for every space. However, today's standards of illumination levels have increased substantially. There are, however, some acceptable standards that should be considered by designers. The table below shows some common areas and the recommended illumination for educational institutions.

TABLE I

LEVELS OF ILLUMINATION FOR EDUCATIONAL SPACES

Type of Space	Foot Candles of Illumination
Classrooms, Study Halls, and Offices	50
Drafting, Keyboarding, Art and Sewing	70
Media Centers, Music and Seminar Rooms	60
Gymnasium, Large Group Instruction, Auditorium and Dining	30
Corridors, Lockers, and Service Areas	20

Lighting may be introduced into educational spaces in various ways. The most common way is use of the ordinary window. However, during the past few years planners and designers have attempted to reduce the amount of glass in educational facilities. Some planners and designers have advocated no windows at all suggesting that having no windows will reduce student distractions caused by the outside world. There are several window arrangements that lie somewhere between these two options. The most promising seems to be the vision strip that runs from floor to ceiling at each end of the room. Another popular alternative is a narrow strip of glass that runs horizontally along the outside wall at approximately eye level for students and slightly below eye level for the teacher. Clearstory windows are being used more and more. Skylights present an entirely different and exciting option. The visual and psychological effect of the skylight can be dramatic with natural light flooding the interior and creating a feeling of warmth and visual comfort. The use of glass block in interior spaces can also allow light to flow between areas.

COLOR

Various colors are used extensively in some schools; many of these colors fail to enhance the environment for learning. The prime factor in color selection should be to enhance the mental, physical, and emotional well-being of students, faculty, and staff. The use of colors for the school should be individualized to suit the particular space under consideration. Planners and designers should be concerned with using proper color to impact the visual environment. Industry uses color to speed production and reduce accidents; hospitals use various shades of color to enhance the effectiveness of the surgeon and to promote faster healing for the patient. Color that is properly used will contribute to an improved environment for learning.

Several colors have a strong emotional and behavioral effect on people and, therefore, should not be used indiscriminately. It has been known for some time, for instance, that blue reduces excitability and helps one to concentrate. Blue is both cooling and tranquilizing. Green has a cooling quality also and acts as a sedative. Yellow, as one might note from the effects of natural sunlight, is cheering and stimulating. It is the luminous color. On dull days, when the yellow of the sun is absent, most people exhibit mental and physical sluggishness and a general lack of enthusiasm for their work; when the sun reappears, they become more active. Yellow also commands attention and so it is used to signal dangerous conditions. Red is exciting and stimulates the brain. Medium red suggests health and vitality; bright red often has amorous connotations. Red also has an aggressive quality and is frequently associated with violence. Purple is perceived as a soothing, regal, and expensive color. On the other hand, orange over stimulates and should be used in relatively small amounts.

The selection of colors for the school should be individualized to suit the particular space under consideration. Palettes of red, blue, and yellow are most popular for kindergarten and primary areas while secondary classrooms and laboratories appear to be most appropriately decorated in palettes of blue, blue-green, green, and grey. In general, guidance activities should be enhanced by warm tints; peach, pink, or turquoise are most desirable for dining areas. Cool or neutral colors should be used for the gymnasium while green, aqua, or peach tints are more appropriate for the auditorium or theater. Rooms facing cool north light should be given warm tones; those facing warm south light should be given cool tones. The front wall of some classrooms can be painted darker than the other walls of the room. A color for this wall should be selected that will be of the same value as the color of the chalkboard so as to minimize eye fatigue. If pastels are used then bright accents can be employed to highlight furniture, accessories, door trims, and doors.

Color has been valued for centuries and has been intuitively used to accentuate certain ends. Educational leaders, planners, and designers who are responsible for educational planning have often virtually ignored the value of color in the learning environment. All of these professionals need to be more concerned with using appropriate color because of its influence on the visual environment and its subsequent impact on the behavior and emotional well-being of the occupants.

FURNITURE

Many educational planners and designers believe that the type of furniture and equipment used in educational facilities plays a major role in establishing the proper environment for learning. Furniture must be conscientiously selected in order to promote an environment conducive to learning. One needs only to review history to see that this has not been the case; for years no thought was given to the selection and upkeep of educational furniture. If coordinated planning of classroom lighting and decoration are to have maximum value for students, then desks, tables, chairs, and other equipment must be designed to promote the advantages gained through proper planning. In developing the concept of a well-designed classroom, furniture is placed high on the list of the important environmental factors affecting the growth and comfort of students. To insure proper bodily function and maintain optimum optical and motor relationships, classroom furniture should be selected properly. Dimensions should fit the student; desk surfaces should be light in color and be arranged to provide both physical and visual protection for students.

In the past, the direction of the educator's emphasis in purchasing was low initial cost; however, more recently, there has been a shift toward better selection of high quality furniture, which costs less in the long run. Consideration should be given to selection of classroom furniture that is flexible, encourages good posture, has safe surfaces, has reflective colors, is resistant to destructive efforts, enhances the appearance of the area, and is durable with minimal maintenance requirements.

There is no all-purpose furniture any more than there is an all-purpose teacher. Thoughtful planning of furniture and equipment can result in elements which relate and harmonize with the building structure as well as coincide with the mechanical and electrical design. The success of a school building as a comfortable, functional, and attractive educational institution will depend largely upon the judicious approach the educational planners and designers take in their selection of furniture and equipment.

THE CLIENT

Sometime during the past few years, planners and designers began to ask, "Who is the true client?" They have determined that it is not the administrators, teachers, or parents but the students. With the student viewed as the key client, it is refreshing to see the resulting innovative designs. Designers who observe students begin to understand the features that are important to students, such as, carpet in corridors, wall graphics, and bells in place of buzzers. It is in the interiors where these individual concerns are a paramount importance. Rather than designing a school that may be institutional, boring, or ordinary, designers want to create an excitement, a dynamism through movement, light, and contrasts of color and form. Good designers pay a lot of attention to the feelings of students. Educational facilities should literally be a shopping mall of educational experiences with classrooms arranged off ramps and corridors overlooking an atrium, plaza, or courtyard. Ramps rather than stairs should be used, where possible, because students like them better.

Sensitivity to these special facets of the interior of schools will greatly improve the learning of young people.

Chapter 8.
Visual Environment

*Kenneth K. Kaestner**

The visual environment provided in an educational facility may be measured by the size of the electrical lighting bill. When energy was cheap no one really worried about how much it cost to provide electrical lighting in a school facility. Electric lighting levels in the 1920s were as low as four foot candles; before the 1973 energy crisis foot candle levels had increased to 70 foot candles and higher. When attention began to center on the increasing cost of energy, electric lighting became one of the possible areas of reduction and conservation. Positive things can be done and were done to reduce the amount of energy used in electric lighting. Programs were instituted by the electric utility companies and others to reduce peak loads and to make the use of electric lighting more efficient. Some obvious measures were to turn off the lights when not in use, reduce the number of lamps in use by removing them, reduce the wattage of lamps, and re-circuit the lighting fixtures so that only one half of the fixtures could be turned on when lower lighting levels were suitable. Some electric utility companies subsidized the changing to lower wattage lamps and encouraged the replacement of lighting fixtures and ballasts to more efficient and lower energy fixtures. In many cases, incandescent fixtures were replaced with more efficient fluorescent fixtures.

Many of the measures taken to reduce the use of electricity for lighting resulted in reduced lighting levels. The notion that lowering illumination levels may reduce the quality of lighting requires attention. Can illumination levels be safely reduced? There is some question whether we need the high levels advocated before the energy crisis. We have reduced illumination levels and no longer do the electrical utility companies advocate higher levels of illumination. In the United States the illumination levels recommended for classrooms are among the highest in the world. The current recommended standard for classroom illumination is fifty foot candles. Forty years ago the standard was thirty foot candles. In this range if the illumination is doubled

---

*Kenneth K. Kaestner is an Architect with Kenneth K. Kaestner and Associates, Modesto, California.

the ability to see is only increased a few percentage points. When the illumination is doubled, the cost of the energy is doubled.

In other areas of conserving energy, heat loss through the walls and windows of the building has also produced fertile ground for improvement in the building envelope. Windows are an obvious candidate for modification due to the heat loss factors. Windows lose most of the heat and since they are expensive and the source of vandalism, there are compelling reasons for the elimination of a troublesome and uneconomic element. There is a convincing argument that if windows could be eliminated, a great savings would result; in fact, the entire building could be put underground and the constant temperature of mother earth would minimize the loss of heat or the gain of heat for that matter. (This has not proven in some climate areas to be worthwhile.) Windows, if used in a limited and careful manner can result in benefit that will far out perform the windowless approach. The windows provide a view of the outside, provide possible ventilation, provide for the well-being of the occupants, and provide for added daylight illumination.

Glare is a universal problem whether we are indoors or outdoors. Try to read outside in the sunlight. Try to see where the sun shines upon the snowscape or the seascape; you can have too much light. Go to a football or baseball game at night and look toward the high intensity flood lights. Try to drive on a rainy night. All of these are problems of glare and accompanying fatigue cause difficulty in seeing. The intensity and the extent of glare is a variable effect and can be measured. It is best described as the difference of the brightness of one surface to another surface. You do not see light; you only see the result of light reflected from a surface. Part of the light is absorbed by the surface and part is reflected. It is the reflected part of light you are able to see. It is the reflected light seen in the classroom that provides the room environment. The goal is to limit the brightness so that the eye does not have to change appreciably to accommodate the light entering the eye where the cone of vision is changed from one focus to another. There are two sources that cause high brightness levels. One is the brightness of the lighting fixtures, and the second is the brightness of the sky and objects outside the room that are seen out the windows, skylights, or clerestories. Any measures used in providing a suitable lighting environment must address and solve the high brightness problem, and the glare that may be produced. The problem of looking outside can be solved by using shades, louvers, or blinds to make it impossible to see the bright sky or other bright objects in the landscape. Another measure is to use dark glass to prevent seeing the bright outside. The glass is very similar to the dark glasses you wear outdoors. Another solution may be to not have windows at all.

When we solve problems the side effects many times should be taken into account. If glare is eliminated with the use of the dark window glass, the inside is affected; the bright sunny day is not so bright and sunny, and the dark stormy day is more dark and depressing. The primary dependence on artificial illumination is adequate and nonvariable and uninfluenced by the outside weather; the entire effect can be monotonous. Some students and teachers are not pleased with the feeling of enclosure brought about by the lack of variety in lighting levels that is experienced with the complete dependence on artificial light. The daylight option affords a more healthful environment supplemented by the natural modeled daylight, the benefit of free light that can be used to reduce dependence on artificial light and provide for windows that can be opened for natural ventilation. In some climates, opening windows can result in lower ventilation and cooling costs. There is hope that the design of school facilities can accommodate the daylight option and can be used to avoid the glare associated with the outside. Skylights are more successful today because they are insulated and watertight, and with suitable spacing and attention paid to roof drainage and flashings they will cause the least amount of maintenance. They provide for top light sources that can enhance the visual environment. Control devices can cause the lights to be turned off should the daylight illumination increase to a preset level. In some cases dimmers are brought in to use without the occupants being aware of the subtle changes in the illumination levels. The savings in electrical usage is sizable and can contribute a significant sum of money over the life of the facility. The use of the top-lighting design allows smaller windows for the outside view, and the reduced window area will help hold down heat loss in the winter. The wall next to the windows is backlighted, and the contrast associated with small windows is reduced.

Where energy codes prescribe the amount of energy to be used in each space, daylighting can provide for higher general illumination levels and allow for more flexibility in how artificial illumination is to be used. In some rooms where more difficult tasks are performed, higher illumination may be required and "TASK" lighting can be employed instead of increasing the general illumination levels.

The use of carpeting on the floors of classrooms and other locations in a school facility is somewhat universal due to maintenance and the favorable acoustical qualities. The carpet is non-reflective and an ideal diffuser. The amount of reflection off the floor cannot be expected to be over fifteen to twenty percent. This causes a problem with the light, both artificial and daylight, because the ceiling should receive light from the floor. This causes the ceiling to be colored by what light comes from the floor, and it causes the contrast between the lighting fixtures if the lighting of the ceiling is dependent upon the floor reflection. The use of computers in school classrooms and laboratories is influenced by the type of lighting system employed. The high brightnesses of some of the direct fixtures causes the fixture reflection to be seen in the screen. The image of the ceiling showing in the screen makes it difficult to see. Attention to the lighting system has been of extreme importance and of even greater urgency because the task is well defined, prolonged, and a source of real pain. The two items, carpeting and increasing use of the computer screens, has changed the way that we use artificial light.

Artificial light fixtures fall into two categories. They are the direct lighting fixture and the indirect lighting fixture. The direct fixture depends upon the light source to shine directly and be seen directly by the eye. The bare lamps are many times shielded from view by shades or by louvres or by the location of the lamp recessed above the ceiling. The bare lamp also can be reduced in brightness by the use of some diffusing medium such as glass or plastic. Some recessed lights and surface mounted lights have high efficiency reflectors that project the light on to prismatic lenses which diffuse the light sideways which spread and even out light. There have been occasions where the diffusers have been removed from the lighting fixture with the idea of gaining efficiency. Lighting systems that depend upon the direct light source shining downward have to depend upon the walls and the floor surfaces to return some of the light to the ceiling surface. There is much to be said regarding a fully enclosed lighting fixture; the factor of utilization is very high because less enters the fixture, and it remains efficient with little or no maintenance except re-lamping. There is another system that is direct and that produces glareless light and is suitable for use over the computer and video screens. This is the luminous ceiling. It consists of lamps located uniformly spaced behind the diffusing plastic ceiling suspended below and concealing the bright lamps. This system is ideal as it is completely uniform in appearance and produces shadowless light. When used in large areas, the eyes are aware of the "sky" and its dominance in the field of vision. It is unvaryingly even and somewhat monotonous. The view of the "sky" becomes tiring. The maintenance of the luminous ceiling is a factor that must be considered since the efficiency of the diffusing element will depreciate due to the accumulation of dust and the change in color due to the aging of the plastic. The cavity above the plastic diffuser gives additional volume in the building and therefore additional expense. This additional volume is required if the system is to provide an even illumination of the diffuser. Classrooms require a ceiling height of at least ten feet to allow for any kind of projection such as slides, overhead projectors, or film projectors. The cavity must be two to three feet deep above the ten-foot level. The direct system only requires a ten-foot ceiling. With limitations on the wattage allowed in lighting systems, the luminous ceiling does not appear to be a suitable solution at this time. In the future, higher output lamps, more efficient reflectors, and prismatic ceiling diffusers may make this system more efficient.

The indirect lighting fixture has the advantage of low brightness; because the light is directed onto the ceiling and the walls above the fixture level. Again the height of the fixture must be at least ten feet to allow projected images. With the ceiling illuminated and no bright or hot spots, the lighting does not depend upon the floor reflecting on the ceiling. The brightness levels are not suitable and cause no glare. The system is viewed by many as not having enough light and is not as efficient as the direct system. Some fixtures allow a small amount of light to shine downward from the bottom of the fixture to give the illusion of the presence of light. This system is about the most visually efficient because of the low intensity of the brightness and the elimination of some of the glare produced by the direct fixture. The indirect fixture suffers from being exposed in the room and is a dust catcher; it also clutters the space in the room and does not have the clean appearance that the flush or surface direct fixture displays. With this fixture the problem of glare and the troubles with the computer and video screens is diminished.

High output lamps of metal halide, mercury, and sodium vapor can be used with fewer fixtures, lowering installation and purchase costs. Light from these fixtures is not full spectrum light and attention has to be paid to the color rendition. The daylight option can help the color modeling and should be used wherever possible to offset the negative effects of this high intensity light. In no case should the fixtures with the high intensity light designed for direct use be used indoors because the brightness may be blinding and harsh

With the design of a suitable electrical lighting and daylight system, color of the walls and ceiling and furnishings is an important part of the entire composition. Many times a good design can be ruined by the color selection. The range of colors used should have a seventy-five percent reflection factor or better. The reflection factors are important; they determine the effectiveness of light that is introduced. If low reflective colors are employed, the light will be "eaten" up and wasted. The use of white chalkboards will improve the visual qualities and reduce the change in brightness in the visual field. These white boards are matte but will pick up the specular reflection from a higher intensity element in the lighting scheme. Where carpet is not used, light color flooring should be encouraged.

Research on the visual enviornment includes studying how the eye functions and what effect the various types of artificial light have upon the ability to see, as well as the possible ill effects caused by the absence of full spectrum light and the flickering connected with discharge type lighting. Studies are also being conducted to predict and design buildings more effectively to use natural light.

The visual environment to be created in a reconstruction or a new building should be part of a total team effort including the architect, the daylighting consultant, the lighting engineer, the mechanical engineer, the color expert, and the furnishings specifier. It is the coordination of these disciplines that determines the final visual environment. The blend of all of the elements—artificial light, the lighting controls, the natural daylight and

and its light controls, and the color surfaces of equipment and furnishings—will determine the ambience of the space and ultimately the quality of the visual environment. We design these school facilities and extend their lives for twenty-five to fifty years into the future. The visual environment demands careful and deliberate attention.

Chapter 9.
Fiscal Planning for Building Projects

*Lloyd E. Frohreich**

Fiscal planning is a complex process that should involve a variety of experts and adequate time to design an educational facility that is economical, efficient, and functional. Hastily planned buildings result in mistakes that affect costs as well as the utility of a building. The purpose of this chapter is to discuss those factors and individuals that should be included in the fiscal planning of an educational facility. In this chapter are discussed those items to be included in the capital budget, the participants in the financial planning process, and the major functions, objectives, and considerations of the financial planning exercise.

Capital Budget

It is important to establish what costs should be included in the budget for capital expansion. Too often one or more of the following is inadvertently left out of a capital project budget.

1. *Acquisition of land* will include costs related to conducting surveys, appraisal, engineering studies, topographic studies, environmental impact studies, legal assistance, purchase, condemnation, removing existing buildings, and relocating existing owners.

2. *Planning costs and architecture fees* will be necessary for most any building project and will include costs to employ an architect, conduct feasibility studies, hire educational consultants, planning and lay committee costs, travel costs to other sites, and extra services required for special engineering studies (structural, mechanical, etc.).

3. *Construction contract costs* will be necessary to cover contracts with general contractors, sub-contractors, construction inspectors, construction managers, legal counsel, bond agents and insurance companies.

Lloyd E. Frohreich is a Professor in the Department of Educational Administration at the University of Wisconsin, Madison, Wisconsin.

4. *Site preparation and development* costs tend to run concurrent with construction costs and will include site drainage, trees and shrubs, landscaping, play areas and physical education fields, black-topping, fencing, illumination, flagpole and any equipment and seating related to athletic fields.

5. *Furnishings and equipment* include moveable and non-fixed items such as chairs, desks, instructional models, fire extinguishers, custodial and ground care equipment, audiovisual equipment, and moveable storage.

6. *Administrative, legal, and insurance* costs will depend on the size and complexity of a project, but usually include expenses related to publicity, postage, accounting, office equipment, legal documents, insurance, and legal and insurance counsel (where not included above).

7. *Contingencies and other costs* should be a part of any building budget and include reserves for emergencies, change orders, unexpected cost increases, and dedication costs. Some experts recommend a contingency of five to ten percent be included in any building project budget.

There were no costs included above for financing debt or debt retirement. It is assumed that the budget needs above will be paid from current revenues, current reserves, or accumulated dollars set aside in a special fund. In fact, many ongoing and minor capital projects require no debt service costs. However, most large building projects do require borrowing and debt service costs. If your school district is one that must borrow, then the following should be included in your capital budget, both short and long term.

1. *Advisory and consultant services* related to the project should include the consideration of a financial consultant and bond counsel.

2. *Administrative costs* will involve bond printing, bond sale and registration, managing debt repayments, conducting a referendum (if required), printing informational brochures, advertising, and public relations.

3. *Debt retirement* includes those costs associated with repaying the principal and the interest on borrowed money.

Participants

The whole area of planning and decision making related to a building project should be under the control of the local school board with the district administrator responsible for advising the board and implementing the board's policies. Most state laws require that decisions about major site purchases, building, and borrowing be made with the approval of the school board and by a vote of the public at a referendum.

Financial planning is important enough to set up a separate committee to consider all of those costs associated with a building project. The school board needs to appoint this committee early in the planning process. The following individuals need to be considered as potential committee members or retained by the school board as consultants at appropriate times in the building project.

1. A *school board member* or two should be a member of the Financial Planning Committee. This person fills the role of school board liaison with the committee and if possible should be a board member with a knowledge of finance.

2. The *district administrator or school business administrator* should represent the central office on this committee. Perhaps both should be appointed by the board. Often, one or the other will chair this committee. Their role on this committee ought to be one of providing leadership, facilitating decision making, fact finding, communication, organizing, and implementing committee directives.

3. The *architect* should serve on the committee if possible or serve as an advisor to the committee. The architect's expertise with respect to estimating costs at various stages of the project is indispensable.

4. A *local citizen* or two should serve on this committee. Someone supportive of schools and with a financial background would be desirable.

5. One of the district's *building administrators* should serve on this committee.

6. A representative of the *teaching staff* should be a part of every building and planning committee. School districts need the support of the teaching staff.

7. *Legal counsel* should be on the committee or serve as an advisor and attend meetings as needed.

8. A *financial consultant* should be retained by the school board to work with the financial planning committee.

9. *Bond counsel* will be necessary if the school district must sell a bond issue.

The financial planning committee should be formed early in the process of planning a building project, for there are numerous building project decisions that need to be made that are related to finance.

Finance Decisions

The decisions made by the finance planning committee and the school board need to be made in the context of a complex relationship between need and the ability of a community to afford a building project. Cost is affected at each stage of the process—from initial surveys and feasibility studies to final occupancy and eventual rehabilitation. It is a false economic concept that the lowest initial cost saves money. True economy is considered by including the variables of original cost, operation cost, and cost of maintenance over time. The goal is to construct the most functional and efficient building for the money over the expected life of the building.

Life-cycle costing is an important principle to keep in mind as a district considers a project's costs. It is a complex concept because of the numerous factors that must be considered and because of the constant change in these factors. Estimates of the initial cost of materials, the cost of maintaining those materials, their life expectancy, and some idea of their replacement costs should give the committee and school board sufficient information to make life-cycle cost decisions. The merits of life-cycle costing are not only that it improves economy over the life of a building but that the analysis develops an awareness of real total costs of alternative materials and systems. No single planning innovation, system, building material, or contractual arrangement will insure an economical building, but when considered in combination, it is feasible to build an efficient, well designed, functional, and cost effective structure.

Financial planning decisions will be concerned with the following areas: (1) developing cost estimates, (2) methods of financing, and (3) obtaining community approval (if required in your state).

DEVELOPING COST ESTIMATES

The budget discussed in the early part of this chapter is an estimate of the costs required to plan, build, and finance a capital project. It is important that the school board, the financial planning committee, and all other involved individuals work closely together at estimating realistic costs for a project. Some very basic decisions will have to be made very early in the planning stages about whether feasibility studies are necessary, whether the district needs educational consultants, whether the district will use a construction manager, the extent and involvement of citizen committees, and the extent and involvement of district staff. Each of these alternatives will result in a different total cost estimate and budget.

With respect to the building itself, there are three stages at which it is useful to have cost estimates. Each estimate is for a different purpose and each is successively more detailed and accurate.

1. A *general cost estimate* is made very early in the planning process and is usually a part of any comprehensive survey or feasibility study. This cost estimate usually is made to answer the question of whether the building project is feasible and whether the district can afford such a project.

2. The *borrowing cost estimate* is more refined and is required during financial planning prior to the building program. This estimate is critical to the determination of the amount of money which will ultimately be required so that planning can begin on sources of funding. It is here that the district will need to decide how much to borrow and what borrowing alternative(s) will be used. The publicity campaign for a referendum (if necessary) is based on this estimate.

3. A *pre-bid cost estimate* is made immediately prior to letting and accepting bids on a project. This estimate is necessary before signing construction contracts and will provide some assurance that cost esti-

mates are still reasonable, affordable, and that the bids submitted are justifiable.

Cost estimates based on square feet, cubic feet, pupil stations or other standard cost measures should be viewed with caution. Often, the cost per square foot or cubic foot does not indicate what space was included in that figure. A cost per pupil or teacher station is seldom a standardized or comparable figure because the needs for different size teaching stations will vary among educational programs and school districts. Still, the most common and reliable figure used is cost per square foot. School districts are advised to look at comparable buildings when making cost per square foot comparisons. That is, if costs per square foot are known, make certain that the buildings being compared are reasonably similar with respect to the quality of construction materials; space features such as the inclusion or exclusion of swimming pools, gyms, cafeterias, auditoriums, etc.; type of mechanical equipment; site development; and space utilization standards. If cost per square foot is used, it is important to use the same method for deriving total square feet for each building.

A satisfactory standard formula to estimate and compare building costs probably does not exist. Cost experts individually projecting the cost of the same building can and do arrive at different figures. Cost comparisons and estimates are more valid when accompanied by a thorough study of construction features, quality of materials and similarity of design components. Cost estimates are more meaningful through a study of building types (structure and materials) and by visiting recently completed school buildings to appraise quality level, design features and costs. School district officials and committee members can more adequately reveal their preferences for design features and construction quality if they see what features exist in other school buildings. Visitations also can help prevent the district from making the same mistakes as other districts.

Assuming a school district has made enrollment projections and knows approximately how many students will need space at various grade levels in the next few years, it is possible to get a rough approximation of both total square footage and cost estimates. National averages, based on information from Architectural Exhibits, reveal the following:

1. High Schools: 150 square feet/pupil

2. Middle Schools: 125 square feet/pupil

3. Elementary Schools: 100 square feet/pupil

With a range of square footage estimates available, an architect should have cost per square foot data available based on current labor and material costs. The estimated cost will be approximately 80 percent of total project costs and includes costs for general contracting, plumbing, electri-

heating, and ventilating. The other 20 percent of project costs will be for site development (not site purchase), built-in equipment, architect/engineer fees, and other fees for legal services, planning, finance consultants, and bond sales. The reader must realize that the cost estimates based on the above procedure are only approximations. The square footage estimates are very dependent on local needs and the types of spaces included in the building. Cost estimates and variations in costs are dependent on the quality of building materials, inflation, and the state of the economy with respect to construction and completion. The very rough approximation procedures and figures given above should be used only in making initial estimates of building project costs.

METHODS OF FINANCING

There are three generally recognized methods of financing the construction of school buildings: (1) capital expansion or sinking fund; (2) current tax revenues; and (3) long-term borrowing, which uses bonds, notes or a state-sponsored capital fund. School districts may use all three forms of financing with larger capital projects. With smaller projects it is more likely that either a capital expansion fund or current tax revenues will be used.

Capital Expansion Fund: A capital expansion fund, or sinking fund, as it is called in some states, is a fund established in anticipation of a building project or several projects. Most states allow school districts to accumulate a sum of money out of each annual budget which is used for future capital projects. Many states also place restrictions on the size of this fund and/or the annual tax rate or tax levy that may be assessed local taxpayers to provide revenues for this fund.

School districts anticipating major expenditures should consider seriously the establishment of a capital expansion fund if one is allowed in your state. Such a fund will avoid or reduce the interest cost on borrowed money and fees and administrative costs related to borrowed money. Further, the money set aside in the fund may be invested and earn interest to offset the costs of a building project. Objections to this approach are that the tax raised is transferred from the private sector (taxpayers) to the public sector (school district) and cannot be used for current capital expenditures. Still, the judicious use of a capital expansion fund can save local taxpayers considerable tax dollars on future tax levies.

Current Revenues: In anticipation of building project costs to be incurred during the year for which the school tax is levied, the school board may wish to increase the proposed annual budget and tax levy to cover all or a portion of such costs. Paying for building projects out of current revenues may be a viable alternative to partially offset the cost of a building or site, but seldom would be appropriate to cover the cost of a major building program. Again, using current tax revenues may avoid or reduce the costs related to borrowing as disclosed in the previous section.

Long-Term Borrowing: Seldom are school districts in a financial position to finance major projects solely from a capital expansion fund or current revenues. The requirements, statutes, costs, and legal implications must be considered carefully when long-term borrowing is needed to finance a building program. It was suggested earlier that if borrowing is imminent, a school district should employ both a financial consultant and bond counsel, in addition to using the district's regular legal counsel. This is an area in which school districts cannot afford to make mistakes. Decisions on long-term borrowing will affect property tax levies and the community for many years.

The alternatives available to school districts under long-term borrowing vary substantially from state to state and an extensive discussion here is not possible. Typically, school districts must obtain voter approval to borrow money over a long term. Many states place restrictions on the length of the bond term for a specific project, size of bond denominations, total outstanding debt, type of bond sold (usually a serial bond is required). Sometimes the maximum interest rate school districts may pay on bonds is restricted.

The Tax Equity and Fiscal Responsibility Act (TEFRA) passed by Congress in 1982 requires registration of all municipal bonds issued as a condition to tax exemption. Registration entails the identification of ownership of the bonds as to both principal and interest on the records of the issuing school district. Payment on registered bonds must be made to the owners of record. This requirement has the effect of substantially eliminating the use of bearer, coupon bonds.

School districts should attempt to:

1. Reduce interest rates by keeping the length of a bond issue low.

2. Seek a quality rating for bonds from Moody's, Standard and Poor's or another nationally recognized bond rating firm.

3. Time the bond sale with favorable bond condition and interest rates.

4. Prepare a detailed bond prospectus with the help of a financial advisor and bond counsel.

5. Market the bond issue on as wide a geographic base as possible.

Many states have funds which school districts may borrow from to finance construction. Normally these funds carry a very favorable rate of interest and their use should be explored before issuing bonds. If the size of the project is not large and local or regional borrowing costs are favorable, districts may want to consider the use of promissory notes or similar borrowing means in lieu of bonding. The feasibility and costs of each of these options should be explored fully.

COMMUNITY APPROVAL

Many states require the approval of the community at a referendum or special meeting for a major borrowing or building program. If school officials have planned well and kept the community informed, and have established a strong rationale for a building program that is backed by irrefutable facts and need, then they will have taken a big step toward obtaining community approval.

There are a few procedures that the financial planning committee should consider as they work toward successful voter approval.

1. Publish and distribute factual brochures that encourage citizens to vote.

2. Form a neighborhood representative citizens' committee that will talk to fellow citizens.

3. Avoid unfavorable votes on issues that are likely to divide the community.

4. Conduct adequate research, analysis, and planning on the building project.

5. Make certain anyone connected with the school district, planning committee, or citizens' committee is kept well informed.

6. Inform the media about the facts and issues of a building program and seek their support.

7. Get those who are inclined to vote yes on a building project to the polls.

Many ideas, concepts, and procedures have been discussed in this chapter regarding the financial planning for a school building project. The space available has limited an extensive discussion of these procedures. Planning to finance a construction project is a major undertaking and requires a major effort on the part of the school administration, school board, and financial planning committee. Anything less will result in mistakes and rejection by the community, as recent years have proven.

Chapter 10.

Construction Management Services

*C. E. Haltenhoff, P.E.**

A construction manager (CM) is a business entity that facilitates the use of the construction management project delivery system on a construction project. The term construction manager is also used to identify individual practitioners who are part of a CM organization.

The construction management project delivery system (CMS) is an alternative to the general contracting system (GCS) and to the design-build system (DBS). The GCS is referred to as traditional in the industry. All three systems utilize the same construction industry resources, but they differ significantly in the manner in which the resources are contracted. The design-build system and the more recent construction management system are both considered to be contracting innovations of traditional construction industry practices. Comparable relationships of the three systems are delineated in Figure 1.

The scope of services provided by the construction manager depends on the CM form and variation employed by the owner. All services must be prescribed in the owner/CM agreement for each project. It is necessary to amend standard documents to include services unique to that project. The basic services are generally included as part of the standard documents. However, it is wise to review these as well since all standard documents are not the same.

The services of a construction manager are identified with the time phases of project delivery: pre-design, design, construction, and occupancy. During pre-design and design, the CM provides services unique to traditional industry practices. In the general contracting system, the input to these

---

*C. Edwin Haltenhoff is Director of Consulting and Research for E&V, Incorporated, Holland, Michigan.

FIGURE 1

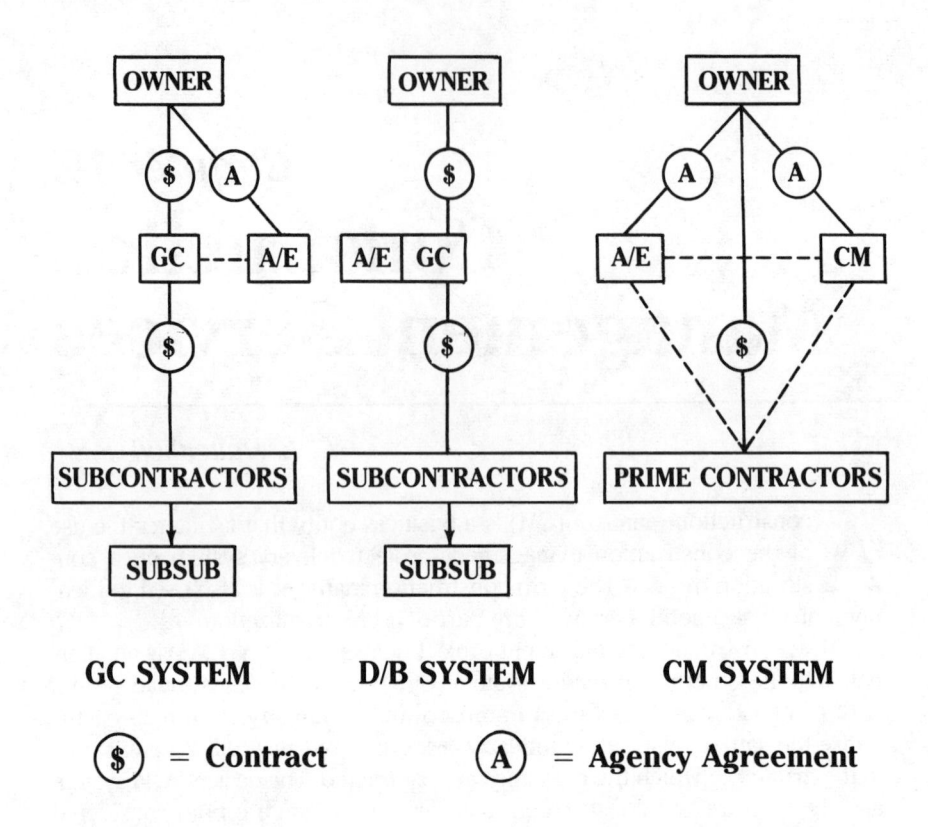

```
GC SYSTEM          D/B SYSTEM         CM SYSTEM
```

OWNER — ($) — GC --- A/E — ($) — SUBCONTRACTORS — SUBSUB
(A from Owner to A/E)

OWNER — ($) — A/E | GC — ($) — SUBCONTRACTORS — SUBSUB

OWNER — (A) — A/E, (A) — CM; ($) — PRIME CONTRACTORS

($) = Contract   (A) = Agency Agreement

phases is design-oriented. The presence of the CM now broadens the orientation to include construction and contracting input. During construction, the CM accentuates the services that are provided by the contractor in the GCS. These services are re-oriented to also benefit the owner in the construction management system. Most CM services extend into the occupancy phase at least one year. This duration coincides with most of the warranties and guarantees stipulated in contractor contracts.

A matrix showing usual CM services is included in Figure 2.

CMS Functions

1. *Cost Management:* Through continuous sequences of budgeting and cost estimating by the CM and evaluations and decisions by the team (owner, architect/engineer, and CM), project costs remain current throughout the design phase and during the construction process.

CONSTRUCTION MANAGEMENT 67

**FIGURE 2
Services Provided by a CM**

	Feasibility	Design	Bidding and Award	Construction	Occupancy
Program Scheduling	*				
Design Coordination		*			
Design Review	*	*			
Value Management	*	*	*		
Value Engineering	*				
Cash-Flow Analysis	*	*	*	*	
Life-Cycle Costing		*			
Estimating	*	*	*		
Budgeting	*	*			
Proposal Preparation			*		
Proposal Evaluation			*		
Contract Documents		*	*		
Contractor Prequalification		*	*		
Expediting		*	*		
Financial Control	*	*	*		
Team Motivation	*	*	*	*	*
Management Control	*	*	*	*	
Contracting Strategy	*	*	*		
Construction Planning	*		*	*	
Construction Scheduling	*		*	*	
Fast Tracking	*	*	*	*	
Site Control				*	
Cost Control				*	
Warehousing			*	*	
Performance Documentation				*	*
Training				*	*
Operation/Maintenance Manuals					*
Facility Startup				*	*
Warranty Coordination					*

The CM must have extensive experience in conceptual budgeting, budgeting mechanics, and construction contract costing. The CM must also have an understanding of the cost of project delivery besides construction costs.

2. *Value Management:* Alternatives, costed by the CM and evaluated by the team, provide the opportunity to inject economic judgment into the design and construction processes, based on requirements, life-cycle cost, expedience, and the time value of money.

CM knowledge of design and mechanical, electrical, structural, and architectural engineering is necessary in order to recommend alternate designs to the team. An understanding of financing, replacement, and maintenance costs is also required.

3. *Decision Management:* The CM team structure provides a forum for decision-making which virtually eliminates actions based on unilateral decisions. When dealing with the complexities of construction project delivey, this management style offers a system of checks and balances not available in the general contracting system (GCS) or design-build system (DBS). The CM system's success depends on a genuine peer relationship between the CM and all other team members. The relationship must be founded on the expertise of the CM in all areas of decision making.

4. *Schedule Management:* Schedule management is a fundamental but comprehensive function of the CM. The goals and particulars of the projects are scheduled in significant detail. The CM must arrange the schedule for the team and contractors.

Computerized scheduling is important for frequent schedule updating. Not only must the CM be an excellent scheduling technician, he must also know what schedules will be effective in every situation. The CM must also understand the time requirements for all phases and elements of construction project delivery.

5. *Information Management:* A CM project must be well-documented. The CM is responsible for documentation in all areas except design. Neither the GCS nor the DBS provides the owner with the quality or depth of information that the CMS provides. Accurate, detailed information aids the owner while the work is in progress and after the project's completion.

The management information system the CM proposed must be an integrated package that contains the amount, quality, and reporting frequency required by the owner. The system must be computerized for frequent updating and easy interpretation. The system should also have sufficient flexibility to permit moderate integration with the owner's installed system.

6. *Risk Management:* A capital expansion project totally relies on the collective efforts of many independent contractors and individual business entities with unique skills. These entities are mobilized for a short period of time to accomplish the construction design created by the architects and

engineers. The necessary and complex interactions of these parties produce a potential for liability. To protect the owner's best interests, it is the construction manager's responsibility to surface, evaluate, and dispose of the risks involved. Although all risks are not financial at the source, neglect would result in serious financial consequences.

The CM must have the resources and expertise to deal with static and dynamic risks. The CM must install a complete risk management program to reduce the owner's potential liability. Knowledge of insurance, bonding, the construction industry, and the elements of project delivery help protect against loss. The owner should realize the transfer of risk is very costly and cannot be complete, but the concept of risk management is an economic alternative.

7. *Control Management:* Project delivery requires the assessment, selection, mobilization, and utilization of many consultants, contractors, fabricators, suppliers, and service organizations. The success of a project depends on the successful management of all these elements. Unlike the general contracting system, where the low bidder automatically becomes the manager as well as the contractor, the construction management system allows the owner to select the CM on the basis of demonstrated management expertise. The CM, as an extension of the owner, provides the expertise to effectively manage the different parties in the construction process.

The CM must have experience in all contracting facets. Some of these include: awareness of contract language and requirements, contract procedures, labor relations, passive and active contract enforcements, liability and property forms of insurance, contracting forms of surety, standards of performance, contractor procedures, construction safety, testing and quality practices, dispute resolution, contractor qualification, purchasing practices, the Commercial Code, design office practice, subcontracting, consultant practices, and other less obvious aspects of project delivery.

8. *Quality Management:* In order to assure that the completed construction will practically and economically serve the owner, the team must establish the owner's quality standards during the pre-design process. During the formulation of the quality standards, the team will call upon the materials and equipment selection experience of the CM.

The CM must then install a quality management plan which accurately reflects the quality standards established by the owner, architects, engineers, and CM. The CM must have extensive knowledge of the functions of both the design professional and trade contractor to develop a quality management program for monitoring design and construction.

9. *Construction/Contractor Services:* Certain forms and variations of the construction management system require the CM to perform some additional contractor services. When an owner selects one of these forms, the CM must have abilities and resources in non-agent areas. The con-

structor forms require CM qualifications that match those of the general contractor. In addition to the fiduciary responsibilities, the CM must be able to handle select projects internally. The contractor forms introduce the additional burdens of subcontracting divisions of work and surety bonds. To provide these requirements, the CM must have sufficient financial strength to hold trade contracts and obtain labor, material, and performance bonds from an established surety. Both CM forms, contractor CM, and constructor CM, depend upon competent CM performance.

10. *Design Services:* One form of the CMS utilizes the project's design professional as the construction manager. It is obvious that the owner's design architect and design engineer will provide CM services under these conditions.

11. *Combined Services:* When combined services are anticipated by the owner, the decision on the providers of each service should be determined independently. Owners must be cognizant that design, construction, management, and constructing services are very different, and qualifications for performance of each are not necessarily connected. If one organization meets the required criteria based on independent evaluations, combined service is appropriate. However, it should be noted that conflict of interest is inherent to the combined services scenario. The final decision should be based on specific project needs.

Activities of the Construction Manager

The specific service activities of the CM consist of the following:
1. The development of the project budget from information provided by the owner and A/E.
2. The design of the management plan and strategy based on the owner's parameters for the project.
3. The scheduling of project delivery from design through construction.
4. The application of value management including direction in constructability and contractability decisions.
5. The formation of contract conditions to facilitate the use of the CM project delivery system, format, and variation.
6. Review of the contract documents prior to issuance to bidders for proposals.
7. The determination of divisions of work to facilitate the multiple bidding process.
8. The prequalification of contractors and the identification of owner direct purchase items.
9. A survey and analysis of the labor pool and contracting practices in the area of the project.
10. Team leadership during the time that the expertise of the con-

struction manager is germane.
11. The development of bidding competition to generate the most favorable pricing conditions.
12. Communication with bidding contractors to clarify conditions and resolve discrepancies in bidding documents.
13. Assistance to the owner during the bidding process to ensure that the receipt of proposals is properly conducted.
14. Review of proposals to determine if those being considered are complete and in the owner's best interests.
15. Leadership in negotiations with contractors on behalf of the owner.
16. Administrative assistance in the signing of contracts and the accumulation of required documentation.
17. The organization and chairing of preconstruction meetings with contractors.
18. The development and implementation of the on-site construction schedule.
19. The coordination of contractors at the site on a full-time basis.
20. The chairing of periodic project and progress meetings with contractors.
21. The establishment and administration of a project reporting system.
22. The institution and coordination of the progress payment procedure for contractors.
23. The procurement and control of construction support requirements for the project.
24. Assistance to the owner and contractors with respect to any labor relations efforts connected with the project.
25. The design and implementation of the project's quality management program.
26. The administration of contract changes and the project's change order procedure.
27. Cost tracking and the administration of the owner's cost accounting program.
28. Assistance in the resolution of disputes arising from the performance of the contracts.

A Concluding Caution

CM services are an extension of the owner's project delivery abilities. By engaging the services of a CM, the owner mitigates but does not transfer the risks inherent to project delivery. The services of CM, though different from those of design professionals, should be considered from the same perspective as those of design professionals and not contractors.

Chapter 11.
Construction Observation

*Douglas L. Johnson**

Construction observation is one of the most important phases of school building construction in which the architect is involved, and this role is critical to ensure that architectural designs and educational plans are molded into the form desired by the owner. Boards of education are probably the least knowledgeable owners that architects encounter because they are drawn from so many varied backgrounds. School board members generally hold those positions because of their interest in the education of children and not because of any expertise they have attained in the area of planning and building school facilities. Board members probably understand less about the architect's role in construction observation than that role in other phases of the building program. Therefore, the contract between the architect and the owner must spell out very clearly what the architect's role is in administration of the construction contract. Many building owners mistakenly believe that the architect performs all supervisory functions associated with a construction project: directing the workers, continuously supervising and inspecting the work, and testing construction materials. The reality in today's legal and economic environment is that architects cannot and do not provide this complete level of service. Confronted with this reality, the owner might then wish to know just what the architect does do other than prepare drawings and specifications.

Fortunately for building owners in general and boards of education in particular, the architectural profession has taken great pains to develop very comprehensive documents, which are published by the American Institute of Architects (AIA), that spell out in detail the role of the architect in the various phases of a construction program. A very good reference document for this information is the "Standard Form of Agreement Between Owner and Architect," published by the AIA. Although AIA documents have achieved a high

---

* *Douglas L. Johnson is Business Manager, Mequon-Thiensville School District, Mequon, Wisconsin.*

level of recognition and acceptance as being fair to both parties, owners would be well advised to have these documents reviewed by their own legal counsel to be sure that there are no inconsistencies with state contract laws and that the documents best serve the interests of the owner. Concerns of this kind can be addressed in addenda to the standard forms.

The standard form of agreement referred to in an earlier paragraph clearly distinguishes between the architect's level of supervision and that provided by the continuous on-site supervisor:

The architect will endeavor by general administration of the construction contracts to guard the owner against defects and deficiencies in the work of contractors, but does not guarantee the performance of those contracts. The general administration of the architect is to be distinguished from the continuous on-site inspection of a project inspector.

When authorized by the owner, a project inspector acceptable to both owner and architect shall be engaged by the architect at a salary satisfactory to the owner and paid by the owner, upon presentation of the architect's monthly statements.

The architect's supervisory duties in a conventional construction scenario would include, but not necessarily be limited to, the following:

1. Establish a schedule for completion of various phases of the project and monitor the job to be sure that established time lines for each phase of the project are met.
2. Supply supplementary drawings for use by the contractors.
3. See to it that all building dimensions are correct as shown in architectural drawings.
4. Assist contractors in the selection of materials and interpretation of specifications.
5. Resolve controversies that arise between contractors or between the contractors and the owner.
6. Prepare change orders when needed and explain those changes to the owner.
7. Approve periodic payments to contractors after verifying that pre-established percentages of the contractor's work have been completed according to the established time lines.
8. Recommend acceptance of the finished building by the owner, and final payments to the contractors.

Since the architect does not provide continuous supervision of all phases of construction, the owner may find it desirable to hire someone to perform those duties suggested by the standard form of agreement. This person is often referred to as a clerk-of-the-works and could be knowledgeable in areas such as architecture, accounting, construction materials, and construction procedures and possess good decision making abilities. It is the job of the clerk-of-the-works to watch for any defects in materials or workmanship that may occur so they can be corrected before they are incorporated into the construction of the building.

The duties of this clerk-of-the-works are more clearly related to daily supervisory tasks than are those of the architect, and may include:
1. Becoming familiar enough with drawings and specifications to be able to interpret them accurately for the contractors and make decisions related to those drawings and specifications without having to call the architect.
2. Preparing a schedule that establishes the time lines for progress by each contractor. This is generally done in consultation with the architect.
3. Inspecting materials to make sure they are provided in accordance with specifications and that they are appropriate for the construction.
4. Preparing periodic progress reports for the architect detailing the status of material deliveries, work accomplished, and other information of value to the architect.
5. Helping the architect determine when periodic payments to contractors are justified based on the percentage of work accomplished in relation to the pre-established schedules.
6. Working with the contractors to preserve the relationships necessary to ensure a cooperative effort on behalf of the owner. This last duty is extremely important because it can prevent arguments between contractors about who is responsible for certain areas where different building trades may be involved.

Some owners do not think it is necessary to hire someone to provide a closer level of supervision than the architect provides, but most authorities believe that board members are not fulfilling their obligation to taxpayers if they do not provide continuous on-site supervision of the construction project. The on-site supervisor can save the owner many times a salary by protecting the owner against defects in workmanship and materials. Once substandard materials have been incorporated into a building or a contractor has been allowed to perform substandard work, the costs to repair the damage that has been done could be quite high and possibly prohibitive. The owner is going to live with the building for many years to come and should be concerned with the long-term benefits of on-site supervision rather than the short-term cost for that individual's services.

In summary, this material has been entitled construction observation rather than construction administration. The terms seem to be used interchangeably in most of the available literature and among those in the construction business but they are different. As noted earlier, owners are generally quite familiar with the role of an architect in translating educational specifications into construction documents and with the architect's role in administration of the construction program. Hopefully, the materials presented above will assist owners in understanding the role that the architect and the on-site supervisor each play in the supervision of construction of school buildings.

Chapter 12.
Construction Administration

Stephen Friedlaender, AIA*

It is essential to the understanding of the roles and responsibilities of the various parties during the construction phase of a project to recognize the fact that the contractor completely controls the action. Upon signing the construction agreement, the contractor assumes the task of staffing the job adequately, of building it according to the construction documents, of supervising the entire work force during construction, of meeting the project schedule, and of completing the project for the contract amount. The construction agreement is between the owner and the contractor; the architect is, technically, not even a party to the contract. As the owner's representative, the architect's job is to provide administration of the contract for construction.

During the schematic design, design development, and construction documents phases, the architect exercises primary control over the direction and pace of the work, and, as the owner's professional advisor, is normally in charge of the bidding/negotiation phase as well. However, once construction begins, the architect is, by the very nature of the work, put into a basically re-active rather than pro-active position.

In many cases, the owner has engaged the services of an architect in the belief that such will be the only professional expertise needed for the duration of the project, and it is often assumed by the owner that the architect's primary role during construction is to keep the project on schedule and to make certain that the work is being carried out in conformance with the contract documents. However, most architects are, by both training and temperament, much more comfortable in the role of creative artist, adviser, coordinator, and synthesizer than as an enforcer of the contract documents, and sub-paragraph 1.5.5 of the *Standard Form of Agreement Between Owner and Architect* (AIA Document B141), which is used as the basis for most

---

*Stephen Friedlaender is a partner in the firm of HMFH Architects, Cambridge, Massachusetts.

Owner/Architect agreements, is quite clear on this issue:

> The Architect shall not have control or charge of and shall not be responsible for construction means, methods, techniques, sequences or procedures, or for safety precautions and programs in connection with the Work, for the acts or omissions of the Contractor, Subcontractors or any other persons performing any of the Work, or for the failure of any of them to carry out the Work in accordance with the Contract Documents.

It must be admitted, at this point, that the *Standard Form of Agreement Between Owner and Architect* and other related documents produced by the American Institute of Architects reflect the time-honored practices and traditions of a profession whose values were formed in a happier and less litigious time when it was reasonable for both owner and architect to assume that the contractor, being a person of integrity and desirous of maintaining a good reputation, would make every effort to construct the project as the architect intended and would need the assistance of the architect during the construction phase only as to the general interpretation of the contract documents and in regard to the working out of technical difficulties which might arise as a result of specific job conditions. As many architects and owners will attest, such an assumption does not, alas, reflect today's realities, particularly as they relate to the administration of construction contracts which are awarded on the basis of public bidding procedures.

Since the majority of school construction projects in this country are carried out by public agencies operating under public bidding statutes, it is essential that those who are responsible for building schools understand "the unique requirements of public projects," particularly as they relate to construction administration. There is some difficulty in generalization due to the fact that public bidding statutes vary from state to state, and the author of this article does not profess to be an expert on comparative law as regards the award of public construction contracts across the fifty states. At the heart of all public bidding statutes is a requirement to advertise the project publicly so that all interested parties may submit bids (i.e., public bidding is intended to be non-restrictive) and to award the contract on the basis of the lowest bona fide bid received.

Taken at face value, there might seem to be nothing wrong with this procedure and, in fact, much to commend it. By encouraging competition from all interested parties and by awarding the contract on the basis of price, the public bidding statutes are designed to keep the selection process free from political influences and to protect the public interest by making certain that the project is built for the lowest possible cost. However, most of us, in our personal or business lives, rarely make important decisions purely on the basis of price. Whether buying a house or an automobile or choosing one airline over another, we are in the habit of weighing cost against other factors such as service, performance record, convenience and even the "personal chemistry" between ourselves and those who are offering their goods and services. The public bidding statutes effectively remove all such factors from the award of public construction contracts and make price the only determinant. There is absolutely no incentive for the contractor to perform the work above the minimally acceptable level because, on the one hand, it might well bankrupt the company and, on the other hand, there is no possibility that the owner or architect could give rewards for a job well done by giving special consideration for return work or by giving a good recommendation to other owners and/or architects. By requiring the public invitation of bids from all contractors who can satisfy the bonding requirements of the project, the public bidding statutes deny to the owner and the architect the ability to limit the bidding to those contractors who have a record of superior performance or to establish effective qualification criteria for bidding. Many states have come around to establishing some sort of procedure for the prequalification of contractors, but in all cases the burden is on the owner or architect to prove that the contractor is *not* qualified rather than on the contractor to prove that the company *is* qualified.

Perhaps the best way to illustrate this is to compare the duties and responsibilities of the architect during the construction administration phase, as described in the *Standard Owner/Architect Agreement,* with the author's own experience in construction supervision of public school projects:

1. Acting as a representative of the Owner during the Construction Phase, the Architect shall advise and consult with the Owner and shall provide administration of the Contract for Construction.

> Awarding public construction contracts on the basis of the lowest bid effectively weakens the architect's control over construction activities by removing whatever leverage or bargaining power traditionally exercised over the contractor's performance. It also forces the contractor to eliminate all non-essential overhead expenses, since large contracts are frequently won and lost by the slimmest of margins. The administration of construction activities is the contractor's major overhead expense, both in the office (in the person of the project manager) and in the field (in the person of the field superintendent), and it is not unusual to find contractors cutting all possible corners at both locations. This puts additional pressure on the architect to perform administrative duties above and beyond those normally expected as the owner's representative. It should be noted that the architect's role during construction is to provide administration of the construction *contract* rather than the construction *process,* and therein lies a major source of misunderstanding. Owners should not expect the architect to become involved in such matters as coordi-

nating the work of the various subcontractors, ordering materials in a timely manner, making certain that there is a sufficient work force on site to meet the project schedule, removing incompetent workers or subcontractors from the job or preventing on-site accidents and taking care of other job security matters. These are the legitimate responsibility of the contractor and the owner should be prepared to take immediate and effective action in the event of unsatisfactory performance rather than asking the architect to take over these tasks.

What the architect can and should do as the administrator of contract for construction is to keep the owner fully informed as to the progress and quality of the work and advise of the need for action if and when the necessity arises. Because it is almost a certainty that there will be matters of contention between contractor and owner, it is mandatory that the architect keep accurate and complete records of all job-related disputes and decisions. This is most effectively accomplished by having the architect conduct all job correspondence on the owner's behalf, by taking the minutes of all job meetings, and by the assuming the responsibility for their distribution to all parties. A complete written record of construction activities is the owner's first line of defense against any possible legal action by the contractor.

2. The Architect shall be the interpreter of the requirements of the Contract Documents and the judge of the performance thereunder by both the Owner and Contractor. The interpretations and decisions of the Architect shall be consistent with the intent of and reasonably inferable from the Contract Documents.

Most construction disputes arise as the result of difference in "interpretation" of the contract documents between the architect and the contractor. In public work, contractors who base their bid on what is *intended by* and/or what is *reasonably inferable from* the contract documents inevitably lose the job to those who base their bid only on what is clearly spelled out in the drawings and specifications. Architects and owners who expect these contractors to give them the benefit of a reasonable doubt when it comes to the interpretation of the contract documents have simply not come to terms with the realities of public bidding. It is essential that the contract documents be accurate and complete in all respects and leave as little room as possible for "interpretation" since the contractor may be expected to file a change order request for anything which he deems to be over and above the minimum legal contract requirements.

3. The Architect shall prepare Change Orders for the Owner's approval and execution in accordance with the Contract Documents.

> As noted above, the filing of change order requests by the contractor is a fact of life on public construction projects. The owner has every right to expect the architect to prepare a highly professional and technically competent set of contract documents but should refrain from considering each and every change order request as evidence of the architect's incompetence, particularly since it is most unusual for a job of any significance to be completed without change orders. Errors and omissions by the architect and/or engineers are by no means the only cause for a change order request on the part of the contractor. Unanticipated latent subsurface conditions frequently result in major changes to the earthwork and/or foundation design of a project, as do hidden conditions in renovation work. It is also not uncommon for an owner to request changes during the construction period, particularly if the project is under budget and surplus funds become available for items which were cut out for budgetary reasons during the design process. Finally, it should be noted that architects who pride themselves on "never having to issue a change order" often have nothing else to offer a client: excessive concern over possible change orders leads many architects to stick with the tried and true and to eschew the truly creative solution. In trying to define what is reasonable, owners should note that many state and local building agencies require that a 5% construction contingency be included in each project budget as a hedge against possible change orders.

4. The Architect shall review and approve or take other appropriate action upon the Contractor's submittals such as Shop Drawings, Product Data and Samples, but only for conformance with the design concept of the work and with the information given in the Contract Documents.

> The careful and prompt review and approval of shop drawings and sample submittals is critical to job progress. Most architects acknowledge that, in today's world, they can no longer limit their review of shop drawings to "conformance with the design concept." They must accept a large degree of responsibility for making certain that the various components of the building fit together and take the time to correct all dimensional discrepancies which may exist. They should not, however, be held responsible for errors on the part of the contractor or for failure of the contractor to make the corrections noted on the shop drawings.

5. The Architect shall visit the site at intervals appropriate to the stage of construction or as otherwise agreed by the Architect in writing to become generally familiar with the progress and quality of the work and to determine in general if the work is proceeding in accordance with the Contract Documents. However, the Architect shall not be required to make exhaustive or continuous on-site inspections to check the quality or quantity of the work. On the basis of such on-site observations as an architect, the Architect shall keep the Owner informed of the progress and quality of the work, and shall endeavor to guard the Owner against defects and deficiencies in the work of the contractor.

> No longer can the architect or the owner assume that periodic on-site observations of the work by the architect will be sufficient to guard the owner against defects and deficiencies in the work of the contractor. The temptation for the contractor to cut corners in order to save money is so great that full-time project representation is essential.

> Full-time project representation can be provided by the architect (as an additional service), by an independent clerk-of-the-works, by a project manager who is employed directly by the owner, by a professional construction management firm or, in the case of large projects, by any combination of the above. The owner who operates under the misconception that no additional supervisory services are needed beyond those provided by the architect as part of basic services is headed for trouble.

6. The Architect shall determine the amounts owing to the Contractor based on observations at the site and on evaluations of the Contractor's Applications for Payment, and shall issue Certificates for Payment in such amounts, as provided in the Contract Documents.

> It should come as no surprise that bankruptcy is distressingly common among contractors and subcontractors who specialize in public work. This is why most public agencies have such stringent bonding requirements. However, the fact that a contractor or subcontractor is bonded does not protect the owner against the possibility that the contractor or a major subcontractor may go under during the life of the project and, at the least, cause a major delay while the bonding company picks up the pieces. For this reason, it is essential that monthly progress payments to the contractor be based upon a careful and thorough review of all completed work as well as an evaluation of all work remaining to be completed. In this, as in the day-to-day observation of construction, the owner's interest will be best served by engaging a

skilled construction professional to act as a full-time project representative to complement the architect's basic supervisory services.

7. The Architect shall conduct inspections to determine the Dates of Substantial Completion and final completion, shall prepare and issue Punch Lists containing the items of unfinished work remaining to be completed, and, upon the completion of all Punch List items, shall issue a final Certificate of Payment.

Under ideal circumstances, the day finally arrives when the contractor notifies the architect that, to the best of his knowledge, the job is complete and final payment is due. The architect is then required to inspect the project in the company of the contractor, prepare a Punch List noting all unfinished and/or unsatisfactory items, and issue a Certificate of Substantial Completion. Substantial Completion is defined as the date upon which the project may be occupied by the owner for the purpose for which it was intended. On school projects, Substantial Completion is the date when classes may begin.

Given the inconvenience and dislocation which may result if a school project is not completed in time for the scheduled opening of school, it is understandable that many new school buildings are actually occupied by faculty and students before they are truly complete. In such cases, the contractor, before releasing the space to the owner, will require that the architect prepare a Punch List containing all items of unfinished work for which the contractor is to be held responsible. This is to protect the contractor from having to repair damage caused by the building's occupants. Punch Lists prepared in such cases are frequently voluminous.

It should be clear from the previous discussion that in construction administration, as in so many other endeavors, the best defense is a good offense. There is very little an owner or architect can do, short of defaulting the contractor, should the contractor turn out to be dishonest or incompetent or both. Under the usual job conditions, the owner's ability to exercise control over the construction process is directly related to the willingness to establish a realistic construction budget at the outset of the project, to give the architect sufficient time and funds to conduct thorough investigations of existing site and building conditions, to prepare an accurate and complete set of contract documents, to set aside a reasonable construction contingency budget under the joint control of the owner and architect to fund the inevitable change order requests, and to provide the architect with professional assistance in the form of a full-time project representative, clerk-of-the-works, and/or construction manager for the observation of construction.

Chapter 13.
Building Remodeling

*Ronald E. Barnes and Richard Diaz**

Many school districts in the past ten years have not been involved in constructing new school buildings, yet educational needs and the utilization of school facilities change. To accommodate these changing needs, most districts have modified buildings, usually changing one room at a time with little or no coordination or master plan.

We will attempt to outline a systematic approach to building renovation while sharing some problems and ideas that a large suburban high school district experienced as it completed an 11 million dollar renovation of two of its three high schools. The projects at the two high schools took more than four years to complete. During this time it was necessary to coordinate construction with instruction in order to enable both the construction project and the instructional program to proceed.

Energy conservation and management should be considered as the renovation project is reviewed. Many school facilities were built when energy costs were much lower and buildings were not designed for energy conservation. Windows, doors, heating, air conditioning, roof insulation, and lighting can all be reviewed for energy efficiency.

Each building that will be renovated was probably built to educational specifications of its respective era of construction. Many buildings that are renovated probably had several additions that were added as the student populations grew. Many of the additions met enrollment needs but sacrificed educational needs.

Our school board operated on a committee structure. One of the standing committees was the building committee. This committee included two board members, the superintendent of schools, the controller (business manager), the district director of buildings and grounds, and two community

---

Ronald E. Barnes is Superintendent and Richard Diaz is Director of School Plant and Facilities, Consolidated High School District 230, Palos Hill, Illinois.

members. The two community members both had expertise that the committee could use. One was a lawyer; the other was an electrical contractor. This committee met almost monthly; during the planning phase of the projects it met more often. It was the building committee's responsibility to interview architects and make recommendations to the board regarding the appointment of an architectural firm to handle the projects. The building committee was also instrumental during the design phase of the projects in determining the scope of the projects and in some cases the specifications on certain aspects of the projects.

The design phase of a project may take between four to six months depending on the size of your project. It is extremely important that staff and user input be included in the design phase. In a remodeling job there are many details that only staff who are teaching and working in a particular area can provide.

The principal of a building should be expected to have the instructional team ready to make decisions concerning the project. Quite obviously, not all staff recommendations can be implemented; however, this input will prevent or solve many problems during construction. Records should be kept of all meetings and sent to all participants. These records will be very valuable during the construction phase. The meetings will also be helpful to the staff because their participation in the pre-construction planning will help them to understand both the process and the inconveniences that may occur during the construction phase of the project. Their understanding of the proposed time line will also encourage contingency planning if the building is not totally ready when school resumes.

If a large remodeling project is being considered, complete room configurations may be changed. A building may have had several previous additions which were constructed to fulfill the enrollment pressures of a given time. Little consideration was probably given to space relationships. Because the construction project could be building-wide, the principal and staff might decide to change the overall space relationships.

The district representative for the project should have a strong background in construction, including heating, air conditioning, plumbing, and electrical systems. This individual should meet on a regular basis with the architects and, once construction starts, with the contractors. Many problems can be foreseen or overcome through this person's expertise. If a district does not have such an individual on staff, consideration should be given to hiring a consultant to handle this coordination.

When an architect is hired it is very important to develop clear understandings as to his expected responsibilities. Architects must always represent the best interest of the district. These understandings must be included in the contract that is signed between the school district and the architect. The district's attorney should review the contract between the district and the architect. It is important not to rely on the architect's attorney for this service.

Weekly job visits and attendance at all construction meetings should be considered essential. Other time requirements of the architect should be clarified; these will depend upon the size of the project and the supervision of school personnel. The more project supervision that can be secured from the architect, the lower probability there is for oversight or construction mistakes.

If the renovation project is expected to be completed during the summer months, it is extremely important to start the design phase early in the fall. This schedule will allow the staff to adequately plan the project and it will give your architect time to design and prepare bid documents.

As bid documents are prepared it is advisable to establish a minimum standard for bonding companies. The quality of the bonding company at times is an indicator of the quality of the contractor. Bonding companies (insurance companies) are rated in the *Best Insurance Guide;* higher rated bonding companies do not readily bond contractors with a bad performance record. A rating of A-15 is the highest rating for bonding companies. Most states require the bidding process. Requiring the high rating may help school districts avoid being saddled with a low bid contractor who cannot deliver.

It is very important that a pre-bid meeting be held with potential bidders. This meeting will allow the potential bidders to clear up ambiguities that may be present in the bid/construction documents. Both the architect and engineer should be required to attend this meeting.

Once the bid has been awarded to a contractor, a pre-construction meeting should be held. At this meeting decisions should be made concerning storage of construction equipment, parking for construction workers, required conduct of construction workers, and optimal time-lines, which will reduce the disruption of school and instructional schedules. A schedule of weekly construction meetings should also be determined at this time.

It is important to develop a firm system for dealing with change orders. Remodeling will cause more change orders than construction of new buildings because there are items that will surface once the contractor has opened up the building. Change orders tend to be over priced because contractors often perceive them as an opportunity to make a considerable profit. Change orders also result in an additional architectural fee, an additional fee to the general contractor, and an additional fee for the subcontractor. The additional fees could be added to the change order which could run as high as 40 percent of the additional work being done. District personnel should bear in mind that the architect and contractor like change orders; they increase profits for both of them. Many boards of education have developed a policy concerning change orders and designating the individual who has the authority to grant change orders. If a policy does not exist, it may be in the best interest of the district to establish such a policy before construction is begun.

It is important that the district's representative participate with the architect and the contractor concerning the interpretations of the specification documents in order to reduce the amount of change orders and expedite the work. In most projects there are certain details that are open for interpretation. Care should be taken to ensure that the district receives what is specified.

It is important to pay contractors on a regular schedule. Contractors generally will allocate their workers to the jobs that pay on a regular basis. It is the architect's responsibility to review and approve all pay-out orders before they are submitted to the district.

The employment of several independent specialists may save the district both time and money when questions develop during construction. An independent engineering firm could be engaged to verify soil quality, fill composition and concrete quality in areas where reconstruction will be performed outside the basic structure of the present building. An independent firm could also be used to verify heating ventilating and air conditioning problems. Air balances and air quantity problems can develop, and it may take specialists to help determine the responsibility for errors in installation or design deficiencies in engineering. An independent firm should also be used if there are serious interpretation problems.

Due to the proliferation of new types of roofing materials available, it is advisable to review this area carefully. Warranties and roof bonds should be reviewed. It is preferable to receive a warranty from the roofing materials manufacturer covering all labor and materials for the full term of the warranty. The fine print should be read to ensure that the warranty does not decline in value each year.

Building reconstruction and renovation, if carefully planned and executed, will provide schools with modern, useful facilities. The students will benefit and the board and the administration will be satisfied knowing that they have provided the students with the optimum learning environment.

Chapter 14.
Relocatable Classrooms: A New Approach

*Robert E. Cascaddan, Thomas E. Ewart, and James L. Schott**

Located in a rapidly growing area this school district is facing projected student growth that could require the construction of fifteen, 24-classroom elementary schools and two high schools during the next five years. Can relocatable classrooms be used to meet the new space needs? Probably. Certain requirements, however, must be incorporated into the design and construction of the units to ensure their equality with permanent construction and to allay common fears of parents that the units are inferior and perhaps give the impression that the educational program is as well.

The facility staff was given the challenge several years ago to prepare a plan for adequately housing students in the burgeoning and changing school system. "Creativity" was the buzz word that triggered the action resulting in staff planning of a prototype classroom design. Research was conducted with educators, architects, engineers, and major manufacturers of building systems and equipment to develop a design program. It was believed that creative professionals could find solutions that combine the best principles of design and construction and develop a new generation of classroom facilities. The job was done. A modern "relocatable" classroom model was created.

Most relocatable classroom units, often referred to as "portables" due to their rather lightweight construction and ease of transport from one site to another, were built in the past as inexpensively as possible. Some were built on a modified mobile home chassis, using an aluminum "skin" on lightweight steel which was hauled into place, anchored, and utilized either singly or in tandem. The wooden portable classrooms are widely recognized and are

---

*Dr. James L. Schott is Superintendent, Orange County Public Schools, Orlando, Florida; Dr. Robert E. Cascaddan is Deputy Superintendent for Support Services, and Thomas E. Ewart is Associate Superintendent for Facilities Services.

relatively easy to move. They are usually constructed off-site and transported by methods used by house movers.

Our school district decided to design a new type of portable classroom—one structurally stronger with a longer "life expectancy." Experience with the wooden relocatables indicated an effective life of ten years with constant maintenance. Frequent movement contributed to this short life span. It was believed that an effective design could be developed which could result in permanent type units (40 years plus "life expectancy") that can be relocated frequently without significant deterioration due to movement. The district's staff completed the design, construction drawings, and the actual construction of 15 such units was accomplished by in-house forces during the summer of 1985. These were to be used at individual schools as needed.

The district's Capital Improvements Section completed the entire task. The project was directed by a staff architect with over 25 years of construction experience. The workers' salaries were incorporated into Capital Outlay funds budgeted for construction. This approach and funding method allowed the flexibility required to hire workers for the project with the opportunity to release them should the workload decrease. Incidentally, the Capital Improvements Section has been in existence for eight years. During all of this time, no reduction in force has been necessary.

The first 15 units were very well received by the schools. They were an instant success. The need for classrooms was great and the demand for these new units was immediate. In order to meet the district's current classroom requirements, it was determined that classroom units would have to be produced at the rate of two per week.

How was the construction process organized? An area at the Facilities Services Compound was cleared and temporary piers of concrete block were constructed which elevate the steel substructures for the individual classroom units. An assembly line technique was adopted. Crews were split into rotating groups, each having an assignment that commenced at the end of the previous classroom unit's completion. From substructure to finished painting, 15 units in varying degrees of completion are continually on site. The temporary foundations simply remain in place for future construction. Following the step-by-step construction technique, when one unit is transported by a School Board-owned tractor-trailer low-boy rig to a school site, construction of another unit on the vacated foundation begins. The outline specifications of the construction materials utilized indicate the quality of the units. It should be noted that the exterior wall surface is a troweled stucco-like finish.

The usual "portable" classroom, with which most school districts are familiar, looks like a small house sitting on masonry piers with the window air conditioning units projecting outside. The design approach for these units resulted in a rectangular building with a nearly flat roof and stucco-type exterior with no projecting utility connections or air conditioning units. The air conditioning system utilizes the familiar unit ventilator which projects slightly into the room but exposes only a flush grill on the exterior. The units themselves are placed on what appears to be a concrete pad at grade elevation. An earth berm makes a 12-inch transition to grade level.

Although the individual modular units are large, encompassing a length of 44 feet by a width of 24 feet, the cost of the units completely equipped is less than $30,000. The prototype units provided an opportunity to make a number of changes such as improved acoustics, glare-free chalkboard locations, cross ventilation, two means of egress, and other interior design features including improved task-lighting, general illumination, and self-contained toilet facilities in each unit. Each classroom is designed to accommodate 30 students, and the cooling requirements amount to three tons. The buildings are so well insulated in all exterior components, including the floors, that three tons of cooling is rarely necessary. The soft, warm tones of the birch interior paneling and the sand colored carpeting, together with brown chalkboards and corkboards, have been selected as being the most pleasing combination of tones for classrooms that will encompass a wide diversity of student ages.

The success of the new individual classroom units was so impressive the question was raised concerning the possibility of constructing an entire school campus utilizing the relocatable concept as the basis for the design. Once again, the design professionals on staff commenced the research. They soon developed a plan utilizing a modular above-ground concrete walk with a superstructure to create a covered walkway that matched the finish of the classroom units. This covered walkway forms a "spine" to connect all segments of the plan. It could provide an above-ground area, underneath the concrete walk, through which utility lines, communication lines, and plumbing lines could be run and would be easily accessible. By constructing the large common elements such as the cafeteria and an administration suite as permanent facilities, the balance of the school could vary in size from eight to 36 classrooms by the addition of units on an as need basis. Cost comparisons between this type of construction and the on-going conventional construction in the school district indicated that at least one third of the cost of a conventional school could be saved with the relocatable concept.

The school district wanted the chance to prove the potential of this new design concept. In order to control the construction process and its costs in such an experimental program, it was considered important to use the in-house construction staff. State law, however, prohibited the use of local employees for projects in excess of $100,000. A special act of the legislature was required to exempt the district from this requirement. Numerous planning sessions and conferences with the State Department of Education officials led to the passage of a special bill and its signing into law by the governor. It allows the school district to construct two modular relocatable classroom schools of 24 classrooms each.

Under the law, the district must continue its study and development of both the design and construction needs. Also, detailed financial records must be kept for the project. Monitoring of the project is being conducted jointly by the State Department of Education and the district. Sites for the schools have been acquired and construction has commenced. Classes will begin in the new schools in the fall of 1987. If the special project proves as successful as expected, it could result in saving taxpayers millions of dollars in school construction costs. This is critical to a growing state.